The Project Management

Memory Jogger™

Karen Tate, MBA, PMP, PMI Fellow
Paula Martin

Second Edition | GOAL/QPC

The Project Management Memory Jogger™
Second Edition

Development Team for 2nd Edition

Karen Tate, Author
Paula Martin, Author
Betsy Hardinger, Editorial Consultant
Danielle Carbonell, Editorial Consultant
Janet MacCausland, Cover & Book Design
Susan Griebel, Proofreader
Monique Mazejka, Marketing

GOAL/QPC | Memory Jogger
8E Industrial Way, Suite 3, Salem, NH 03079
Toll free: 800.643.4316 or 603.893.1944
service@goalqpc.com
MemoryJogger.org

Printed in the United States of America
Second Edition   10 9 8 7 6 5 4 3
ISBN 978-1-57681-122-1

Acknowledgments

We thank the following people for their comments, knowledge, and inspiration throughout the development of this product.

Matthew Booth &
Pam Burton
Scudder Stevens & Clark

D'Anne Carpenter &
Diane Evangelista
Mercy Health Services

Roland Chapell
Northrop Grumman

Charlotte Chase
New Venture Gear, Inc.

Mark Daniel
Inco Ltd.

Ellen Domb
PQR Group

Kathleen Donohue
School House Consulting

Connie Emerson
CJM Associates

Susan Engelkemeyer
Babson College

Bea Glenn
Chiquita Brands International

Betsy Hardinger
Editorial Consultant

Dave Haskett
Johnson Controls, Inc.

Susan Hillenmeyer
Belmont University

LuAnn Irwin
Eastman Kodak

Paul Jones
Procter & Gamble

Rod Lincoln
Cytec Industries

Janet Payne
Alliance Blue Cross/Blue Shield

Nancy Pope
Nestlé USA

Rich Rischling,
GE Capital Real Estate

Diane Ritter
GOAL/QPC

Michael Schneider
Lucent Technologies

Steve Schneider
Rhone-Poulenc
North American Chemicals

W. Charles Slaven
The Kroger Company

Larry Smith
Ford Motor Company

Frank Tenne

Paul Tremel
HDR Engineering

Melba Watts
AT&T

Peter Whiting
Rank Xerox Ltd. UK

About this Book

The Project Management Memory Jogger™ was written by Karen Tate, PMP, and Paula Martin and first published by GOAL/QPC in 1997. Since then it has become an indispensable resource to tens of thousands of people working with projects, on project teams, and project managers who made the first edition an international best-seller.

This second edition retains the essential features that made the first edition so popular and is aligned with *A Guide to the Project Management Body of Knowledge* (PMBOK® Guide). In addition to all of the steps, proven tips, tools and templates, the new edition features new sections on

- ○ Project Communication Plan
- ○ Cross Cultural Teams
- ○ Project Procurement Plan
- ○ Project Quality Plan
- ○ Organizational Change Management
- ○ Project Contingency
- ○ Projects vs Operations

and expanded segments on working with teams, virtual team tips, scope (customer analysis and SMART Criteria), risk, scheduling (critical path), monitoring & control, (earned value), and many more additions.

Finally, there is a new section on consensus based decision making tools to help project teams from *The Memory Jogger*™ *2 Second Edition*. In addition, the overall flow and layout have been improved to make this new version even more user-friendly than the first.

We hope that this improved guide will help you get the most out of your meeting time and also help to improve the success rate of projects in your organization!

The method described in this book was developed by the authors to help simplify the process of moving a project successfully from concept to completion. It is consistent with industry standard approaches such as PMBOK® Guide, with an emphasis on participation, empowerment, individual accountability, and bottom-line results. It utilizes tools and concepts from continuous process improvement and applies them to making project management accessible to anyone working on a project.

About the Authors

Karen Tate, PMP®, MBA, PMI Fellow, is founder of *The Griffin Tate Group, Inc.* (TGTG), a charter Global Registered Education Provider of the Project Management Institute. TGTG provides project management training and consulting for every one in the organization associated with projects—project managers, project team members, project sponsors, and senior managers. She has over 25 years of domestic and international experience in project management and is the co-author of numerous books on the subject.

Paula K. Martin is the founder of, and executive consultant for, *Martin Training Associates*, a management consulting and training firm specializing in basic and advanced project management skills; and in the tools and processes needed to create an enterprise-wide system of innovation. Martin Training is also known for its highly innovative approach to managing a matrix organization, known as Matrix Management 2.0. Paula is the author of over 10 books, including *The Innovation Tools Memory Jogger*™, which provides today's project leaders with the tools they need to be tomorrow's innovation leaders. Paula can be reached at **pmartin@martintraining.com**.

Introduction

Welcome to the second edition of *The Project Management Memory Jogger*. This edition has been significantly updated. First, you'll note that I describe the new tools and techniques that have been developed during the past decade to help project managers successfully guide project teams. For example, we have included new sections on additional knowledge areas from *A Guide to the Project Management Body of Knowledge* (PMBOK® Guide)—*Fourth Edition*.

The PMBOK® *Guide* is the global standard for project management published by the not-for-profit Project Management Institute (PMI). PMI® is an international professional association dedicated to advancing the practice, science, and profession of project management. Founded in 1969, they now have more than 400,000 members in more than 140 countries. For more information, see **www.pmi.org**.

Increasingly, the members of project teams are working in offices scattered throughout the world. They "meet" only by telephone, teleconference, or e-mail, and they experience special challenges in working together while working apart. In this edition, you'll find tips and techniques specifically designed to address the needs of these virtual teams.

How to Use This Book

This pocket guide provides a variety of examples, visual cues, design features, and clear, friendly language that we hope will encourage project teams everywhere to use this book, and use it often. Everyone on a project team can use this book as a daily reference on the job or as a supplement to training. Have fun!

To Find a Topic

Use the contents pages that follow, or consult the chart at the beginning of every chapter (shown below).

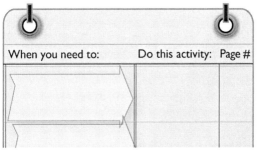

When you need to:	Do this activity:	Page #

To Find the Start of Each Chapter

Look for the solid box at the bottom of the page.

To Find Tips

This edition also contains tips for face-to-face, as well as virtual team situations. Tips are noted by this icon.

To Find Illustrations of the Book's Case Study

Look for the flip chart pad with graph paper or 3-hole punched paper. The case study follows a project team as it plans and executes an off site 3-day conference on—you guessed it—project management.

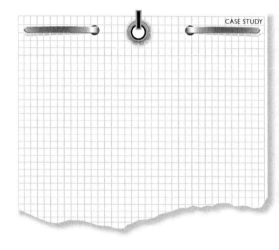

CASE STUDY

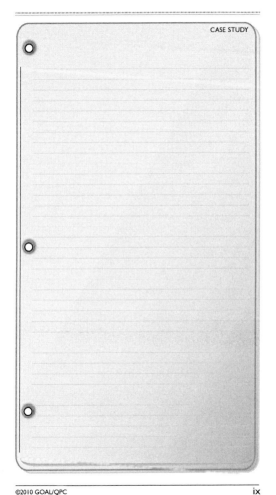

Initiation

2

- Develop a charter
- Define the big-picture scope
- Define the project's limits

CHARTER

Working with the Team

3

- Lead the Team
- Hold effective meetings

The Project Management Memory Jogger™ 2nd edition | ©2010 GOAL/QPC

Table of Contents

Leadership Summary

Why do organizations need project management?

Project management . . .

- Ensures that customer requirements are met.
- Eliminates reinventing the wheel by standardizing routine project work.
- Reduces the tasks that might be overlooked.
- Eliminates duplication of effort.
- Ensures that projects are under control.
- Maximizes the use of resources.
- Minimizes rework.

What is involved in the project management process?

- o The organization decides to launch a project.
- o The project charter is prepared by any of the following: the project sponsor, the project manager, or the management steering group. The project charter outlines the requirements, objectives, and limitations of the project.
- o The project charter is discussed with the project team and project manager, and then it is distributed to management and key project stakeholders.
- o The project team and project manager draft a project management plan. This plan is approved by the project sponsor and distributed to management and key stakeholders.
- o The project management plan is executed and monitored, and the final deliverable— a product, service, process, or result—is delivered to the project customer(s).
- o The project team, project manager, and project sponsor evaluate the project, write a closeout report, and distribute it to management and key stakeholders.

Who Has Project Accountability?

Person or group	Is accountable for . . .
Senior Management	Ensuring that the organization has a project management process that project teams can follow.
	Providing the resources to support selected projects.
Functional Manager	Providing resources from her area to support the project.
	Supporting the project objectives.
Project Sponsor	Initiating the project.
	Ensuring that the project has clear direction and support.
	Providing a project charter to the project team.
	Ensuring that the project satisfies the customer as well as the organization.
Project Manager	Ensuring that the project management plan meets the requirements of the project customer.
	Leading the project team.
	Ensuring that the project satisfies the customer as well as the organization.

	Ensuring that the project is completed on time and within its limits and constraints.
Project Team Member	Completing his assignment to create specific deliverables or perform a defined function.
	Ensuring that his part of the project work satisfies the requirements of the project and is completed on time and within budget.
Project Customer	Representing (or being) the user.
	Providing requirements for the deliverables.
	Making decisions as needed.
	Producing assigned deliverables.
	Accepting the final deliverable.
Subproject Leader	Meeting subproject objectives: scope, cost, and schedule.
	Leading the subproject team.
	Planning and executing the subproject.
	Monitoring and reporting subproject team progress.

You Are HERE

1

Chapter

Chapter

ONE

CREATING SUCCESSFUL PROJECTS

A *project* is "a temporary endeavor undertaken to create a unique product, service, process, or result" (PMBOK *Guide*, 4th edition). A project can be as simple as the plan for an off-site retreat or as complex as the construction of a medical center. The project team can range from a few people to hundreds or even thousands, and team members may work in one location or across continents.

Projects bring together people from a range of jobs to collaborate in a unique way. A project's *stakeholders* are individuals or groups that need to be considered when you make decisions and will be affected (positively or negatively) by the project.

Because projects are diverse and flexible, organizations increasingly use them as the preferred way to fulfill the needs of customers.

What Is a Successful Project?

All project teams can judge the success of their projects in the same way:

- ○ The project customer is satisfied or delighted with the final deliverable (a product, service, process, or result).

- The deliverable is given to the project customer on time.
- The project team has met the project objectives of scope, schedule, and cost.
- Project team members have increased their skills and knowledge as a result of the project.
- The organization has benefited from the lessons learned by the project team.

How Do Projects Relate to Your Organization's Strategy?

Most organizations operate under an annual or periodic *strategic plan*—a description of how (and even why) the organization will meet its goals, which typically involve maximizing profits by increasing revenue or reducing expenses. Projects are one means of implementing a strategic plan. Before a project is launched, an organization examines its business opportunities and, guided by the strategic plan, evaluates these options using a cost–benefit analysis or similar assessment. The organization then selects projects for implementation and appoints a project sponsor to oversee or be accountable for it.

What Is Project Management?

Project management gives project teams a process that helps them coordinate their efforts so that they can create the right deliverable at the right time, for the right customer, within the resource limits established by the organization.

Project management was once the exclusive job of professional project managers, who most often coordinated the activities of specialized, complex, large-scale projects. In recent years, however, the role of project managers and project management has been changing.

Companies have applied project management to a broad range of projects, from simple to very complex, and from manufacturing to service and education and a host of other areas. Based on the success of the project management approach, the people who lead and work on projects today are not necessarily trained project managers. They have various backgrounds and experience.

Although project managers still have an important role to play, all the members of a project team are expected to understand, participate in, and carry out a project by performing project management activities. *The Project Management Memory Jogger* is all about project management as a *participative process*—a process that includes all the team members in developing the project management plan to get better information and buy in. This book's structure, details, and tips are all designed to help project team members and their project managers learn to do it better.

How Does Project Management Help Project Teams?

Why should you use a clearly defined project management process? After all, some people might argue, projects usually turn out OK, and the deliverable typically is acceptable. But the question is, At what cost? Here are some of the typical problems that project teams experience when they don't use a project management process.

- ○ Workloads for some individuals become excessive.
- ○ The project has cost overruns.
- ○ Team members lack the right skills or expertise for the project.

- There are staffing conflicts with other projects or assignments.
- Relationships among team members are strained.
- The scope of the project keeps changing.
- Work is duplicated or must be redone.
- Resources are insufficient.
- Deadlines are missed.

Your project team doesn't have to get trapped in these pitfalls. This Memory Jogger™ describes a simple, easy-to-use process for managing projects.

Using this process helps you avoid the typical time-wasting mistakes that hinder projects and instead enjoy successful project outcomes every time.

Getting Ready

Before you start your project, you and your project team should take time to review the key terms you will encounter. These terms, shown in the following table, are critical to your understanding of the key concepts in this book.

Key Terms

Project	A temporary endeavor undertaken to create one or more deliverables—a unique product, service, process, or result.*
Project management	The application of knowledge, skills, tools, and techniques to project activities to meet the project requirements.*
Deliverable	Any unique and verifiable product, service, process, or result.*
Interim deliverable	A deliverable produced during the process of creating the final deliverable.
Final deliverable	The deliverable given to the customer of the project.
Organizational deliverable	A deliverable that is intended for the organization, not the customer.
Operational deliverable	Benefit the project will deliver, often the reason for the project. The process owner (and not the project team) is accountable for delivering the results as part of normal business operations.
Resources	Time, effort, money, equipment, and so on required by or for the project.
Risks	The potential for problems to occur on a project.
Subproject	A smaller piece of a project created to make the project easier to manage. Led by a subproject leader.

* Starred terms are adapted from A Guide to the Project Management Body of Knowledge (PMBOK® Guide), 4th Edition (Newtown Square, PA: Project Management Institute, 2008).

For more details on the various kinds of deliverables, see page 72 in Chapter 4.

A deliverable is a noun, not a verb. It is something you produce. An *activity* is something you do.

Who's Who in Projects

Project Sponsor

The *project sponsor* is a key leader and a liaison between management and the project team. The project sponsor's role is to initiate the project by creating a *project charter* (Chapter 2). The project charter is the foundation of the team's planning process. If the project sponsor does not complete the project charter, then the project team must create it and get it approved by the sponsor.

Project Team

After the project charter has been created and approved, the project team is formed and meets for the first time. In this session, project team members agree on the ground rules and meeting guidelines that they will follow throughout the project (Chapter 3). Next, the project team develops a *project management plan* (Chapter 4), and then it executes the plan (Chapter 5). As a last step, the team closes out the project (Chapter 6).

Project Manager (or Subproject Team Leader)
- Facilitates the project process
- Collaborates with the team to create and execute the project plan

---

    ○ Monitors and reports the progress of the project to the project sponsor

    ○ Resolves project issues

 Subproject leaders have the same responsibilities for their subprojects as the project manager has for the project.

Project Team Member

    ○ Ensures that his part of the project work gets completed on time

    ○ Acts as a liaison with a supervisor or subproject leader

    ○ Monitors and reports the progress of his work on a subproject

Projects Versus Operations

It's important to distinguish a project from *operations, or business as usual*. Operations are supported by an infrastructure: organizational charts, roles and responsibilities, policies, procedures, processes, and so on. In contrast, *projects* may not have this infrastructure. So in addition to the work of the project, the project team may need to create the project's processes, define the roles, and so on.

How Projects Differ from Operations

Projects:	Business Processes or Operations:
• Temporary; one-of-a-kind	• Permanent; mass-produced
• Unique output	• Repetitive output
• No preassigned jobs	• Job descriptions and assignments
• For many projects, the processes that produce the deliverables must be created	• The deliverables process and technical processes are clearly defined, documented, refined, and continuously improved
• Different inputs each time	• The same inputs or supplies each time
• Not part of the permanent structure of the organization and may not be part of the annual performance evaluation of individuals	• Part of the permanent structure of the organization and part of the annual performance evaluation of individuals
• May require the development of a project management methodology	• Part of a periodic planning cycle and standard process
• Project duties may not be part of each individual's performance evaluation and compensation, and may interfere with performance ratings	• Job duties are the basis for each individual's performance evaluation and compensation

These differences explain why projects tend to be riskier and less efficient than regular business operations, and why many business managers have unrealistic expectations for projects. They are more familiar with operations, where risks tend to be lower and more predictable, efficiency is higher, and rework is lower.

Additionally, organizations earn revenue through normal business operations, but the benefits of projects, including any increases in revenue, lie in the future. Thus, when a project needs resources, support, or priority, managers may view it as a drain on human resources and an interference with business operations. The organization doesn't immediately feel the consequences of denying or delaying resources to a project.

Uncertainty (risk) tends to be higher for projects than operations. Efficiency and productivity tend to be higher for operations than projects.

How Projects Work

The sequence of major project management tasks that a project team must complete, from the chartering of the project through project closeout, is essentially the same for every project—whether the project is simple or complex or involves a few people or many people. But within each major task, projects can take various paths based on their scale or complexity. What's important is to do no more and no less than is required by the project management process, depending on what your project requires.

The road map on the next page charts the course of any project. The signposts point you to the details of each chapter so that you and your project team can move efficiently toward your final destination: a successful project!

You Are HE

1

Cha

A Project Road Map

You Are HERE

1

Chapter

Initiation
- Develop a charter
- Define the big-picture scope
- Define the project's limits

2

Working with the Team
- Lead the Team
- Hold effective meetings

3

Developing the Project Plan

4

- Add details to the project scope
- Determine project boundaries
- Estimate schedule, budget, and staffing
- Analyze risks and identify risk responses

5

Execute the Project
- Monitor and report project progress or status
- Manage changes to the project

6 Close Out the Project
- Evaluate the project
- Prepare closeout report

Project Management at a Glance

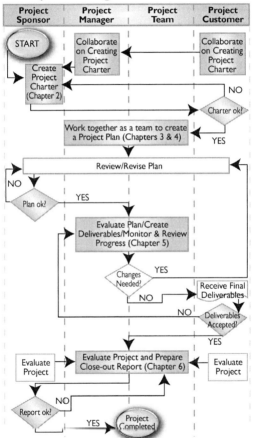

1 | **Creating Successful Projects**   11

The Project Process

As the road map shows, it's useful to think of a project in four major segments:

- Initiation
- Planning
- Execution
- Closeout

In addition, project monitoring and control occurs throughout the project, although it's concentrated mainly in planning and execution.

After this introduction, Chapter 2 covers project initiation. Chapter 3 is about working with a team, face to face or virtual. Project planning is explained in Chapter 4, and project execution is covered in Chapter 5. You'll find project closeout in Chapter 6.

Let's take a brief look at these project elements.

Project Initiation

To initiate a project, you follow the process of *project initiation* to gain authorization for the new project. This process ensures that the project manager, project team, project customer, and project sponsor understand the goals and constraints of the project in the same way.

The deliverable of project initiation is the project charter, which documents and formally authorizes the project. The project charter outlines the project's high-level objectives. The project sponsor, project initiator,

---

or project manager may write the project charter; it is usually approved by the project sponsor.

Project Planning

The purpose of *project planning* is to document and formally approve the resources required to achieve the project objectives within project constraints. In project planning, the project team produces the project management plan.

The *project management plan* is a formal, approved plan that documents how the project will be executed, monitored, and controlled. It is written by the project manager and project team members and approved by the project customer and project sponsor.

 To determine how much planning is appropriate for your project, see the table on the next page.

The chart on the next page details an at a glance summary that shows how the level of project management affects project attributes.

How Much Project Management?

Project Attribute	More Project Management (Large, Critical, or Complex Projects)	Less Project Management (Small, Simple Projects)
Schedule	Schedule contains milestone dates, interdependencies of deliverables, and detailed activities.	Schedule contains only milestone dates.
Cost budget	Cost estimates contain detailed estimates both of internal costs (i.e., employee labor costs, internal charges) and external costs (i.e., subcontracts and purchase orders).	Cost estimate is not itemized.
Staff effort budget	Labor budget contains detailed estimates of effort hours by activity.	Labor estimate is a single, imprecise number based on past experience or the number of people and duration of tasks.
Risk analysis	Risk analysis is always current and contains probabilities and impact or decision-tree calculations, along with risk triggers and budget and schedule contingencies.	Risk analysis contains a brief list of the risks and planned responses or countermeasures.
Communications	Communications involve an elaborate communications plan (who, what, how, and when).	Communications include a basic communications plan or status report.
Scope	Scope is fully developed, and all deliverables are adequately defined.	Scope is limited to a list of deliverables with acceptance criteria.
Procurement	Procurement plan contains a list of planned subcontracts and purchase orders, including costs and lead times, expediting, and quality assurance plans.	Procured items are included in the cost estimates and schedule dates. There is no separate procurement plan.
Project controls	Status reports include risk, cost, schedule, effort, issues, and earned value analysis.	Status reports include actual completion dates, costs and effort, and issues.

The Advanced Project Management Memory Jogger™

Project Monitoring and Control

This is the process of tracking, reviewing, and adjusting project performance to meet project objectives. Its purpose is to ensure that the project deliverables meet the customer's acceptance criteria and the project objectives. It is used throughout the project, most heavily during execution and next most heavily during planning.

Project Execution

Project execution is the process used to execute the project management plan to meet project objectives. During this phase, the project team performs project work, provides status information, and produces deliverables. The project manager directs and coordinates the execution of the project.

Project status reports are delivered to management. These reports document the status of the project work and outline proposed actions to resolve any differences between the status and the plan. They are prepared by the project manager and project team.

Project Closeout

Project closeout is the process used to finalize and formally complete the project. In project closeout, the team verifies the work of the project and ensures that the project customer and project sponsor accept the work.

The project team does the following.

- ○ Measures customer satisfaction
- ○ Documents lessons learned
- ○ Provides recommendations for improvement
- ○ Archives project documents
- ○ Communicates lessons learned to the appropriate parts of the organization

The main deliverable of closeout is the project closeout report. This report to management documents the final project status and results. It is prepared by the project manager and the project team, and in some cases, the customer. When it is completed, the closeout report is delivered to the project sponsor and team, along with the office of project management, if one exists.

Initiation
- Develop a charter
- Define the big-picture
- Define the project's limi

CHARTER

2

Working with
the T

Chapter

TWO

HOW TO INITIATE YOUR PROJECT WITH A PROJECT CHARTER

New projects should be initiated with a project charter. The *project charter* documents what the project sponsor wants the project to achieve as well as the project's limits and constraints. This process ensures that the project manager, project team, project sponsor, and project customer understand the goals and constraints of the project in the same way.

After the project team does additional planning, the team may determine that some of the items in the charter need to be negotiated.

A key term to know is *deliverable*. A deliverable can be a product, service, process, or result. Examples of deliverables are a design package, a sales meeting, a plan for process redesign, or a product prototype. The deliverable (or output) of project initiation is the project charter.

Anything produced for the project customer is a *final deliverable*. Anything produced along the way is an *interim deliverable*.

The project charter is written by at least one of the following: the project sponsor, the project manager, the project team, or the project initiator. It is usually approved by the project sponsor, the project initiator, or the project customer (or all three). The project manager should hold a discussion with the project sponsor or customer (or both) about the information to be included in the charter. If the sponsor and customer are not available, then the project team should complete the charter using the best available information and verify it before proceeding to planning.

Every project needs a charter. If the project sponsor doesn't provide it, the team should create it and get it approved.

When you need to:	Do this activity:	Page #
Describe the business opportunity or problem, identify project customers and acceptance criteria, and specify the strategic goals of the project (the project priorities)	Define the Project's Scope	19
Define the maximum desired risk (risk limit) for the project and the project's reviews, approvals, and reports required	Complete the Project Assurance Section of the Project Charter	27
Define the allowable resources (time, money, people, and so on) and constraints of the project	Complete the Resources Section of the Project Charter	29
Ensure approval of the project charter and communicate project information to stakeholders	Review, Approve, and Distribute the Project Charter	33

If your organization has an archive of project charters and lessons learned from earlier projects, review these materials with your team as you begin your project.

Define the Project's Scope

Why do it?

To describe the business opportunity or problem the project is designed to address, as well as the project's deliverables, its customers, and the customers' requirements for the final deliverables. If team members have a clear understanding of the project scope, they will be better able to satisfy the customer. The scope section also identifies the key stakeholders and describes any organizational deliverables.

 This part of the chapter gives you a general description of how to outline the project's scope in the project charter. For a more detailed discussion of developing the project scope for the project management plan, see Chapter 4.

How do I do it?

1. Give the project a name.
   - ○ Choose a name that reflects the purpose or anticipated final deliverable of the project.

2. Describe the business problem or opportunity.
   - ○ Describe the business environment if applicable.
   - ○ Explain how the final deliverable will solve the problem or exploit the opportunity.

Tip

Most projects fall into one of the following categories:
- Increase revenue or market share via new or improved products
- Decrease expenses or costs
- Increase efficiency or throughput

CASE STUDY

Project name: *3-Day Conference on Project Management*

Problem/Opportunity: *Project managers, team members, sponsors, project customers, functional managers, and others who work on projects need a better understanding of their roles on projects and current best practices.*

3. Identify the project customer or customers.

    ○ The project customer either uses the final deliverable or represents the users of the final deliverable.

    ○ Determine who will approve and use the project's final deliverable.

    ○ The project customer may be internal (part of your organization) or external (outside your organization).

- If the project has more than one customer, clarify exactly which function, area, or decision each controls or owns. Obtain agreement, document, and publish.
- Ask for customer acceptance criteria, and apply the SMART technique: make the criteria Specific, Measurable, Achievable, Realistic, and Tangible. For more on this, see Chapter 4.

Project Results Versus Operational Results

Sometimes the project sponsor or project customer describes the final deliverable as an operational result: "The project should produce a 15% decrease in costs in area X." In this example, the final deliverable is a new or improved work process or procedure that is **capable of producing** the 15% decrease in costs; the process owner or manager of that area is accountable to operate the process correctly to achieve the operational result. In this situation, the project team can rephrase the final deliverable as "a process that is capable of delivering a 15% decrease in costs of area X."

Include a pilot test to verify whether the savings can be achieved. And make sure it is clear that the "proven" improved process is formally turned over so that operations owns the process and is accountable for the operational results.

For internal projects, the project sponsor and project customer may be the same person. For multiple customers, see Chapter 4.

4. Rank the project decision criteria: faster, better, or cheaper. + more sustainable?

- ○ As a baseline, assume that the project will meet the project objectives, the deadline for the final deliverable, project spending limits, and acceptance criteria for the final deliverable.

- ○ Then prioritize those three factors—scope, schedule, and cost—as first, second, and third to help the project team make decisions that require trade-offs. This ranking is based on the project sponsor's and customer's priorities for the project.

- ○ Another way of thinking about trade-offs among these three elements is to ask, What's most valuable to the project—faster, better, or cheaper?

"Faster" (the schedule) would be the first priority if an earlier launch of a new product or improved process would impact the expected revenue or savings to the organization.

Remember that the project decision criteria set priorities *within* the project, *not* the priority of this project compared to other projects.

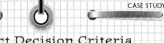
Project Decision Criteria
for 3-Day Conference

"Lower cost" is given the highest priority because the conference is a major profit-generating event for the organization.

"More features" is given the second highest priority because the quality standards for the conference are already high and adding more features will not significantly increase the value of the conference for the participants.

"Earlier delivery" is given the lowest priority because the dates of the conference are fixed.

Priority	Rank
Lower cost	1
More features	2
Earlier delivery	3

5. Briefly outline the project customer's requirements.

 ○ Determine the problem the project customer wants to solve by using a specific final deliverable.

 ○ Find out whether the project customer is looking for specific features or has defined specifications for the final deliverable.

 ○ List the features or functions of final deliverable.

The project sponsor may not know the project customer's requirements, so the sponsor may delegate this task to the project team.

6. Describe the final deliverable(s).

  ○ The final deliverable is a product, service, process, or result.

  ○ It is delivered to the project customer.

  ○ It must satisfy the customer's requirements.

  ○ A project usually has only one or two major final deliverables.

  ○ If more than one option would satisfy the project customer's requirements, the project manager or the project team should work with the project customer and/or sponsor, if possible to finalize the deliverable.

  ○ A large project may refer to the final deliverable as a "system" rather than treat each element separately.

7. Describe the acceptance criteria for the final deliverable.

  ○ List the criteria that the project customer will use to accept or reject the final deliverable. Whenever possible, ask the customer to provide these criteria.

  ○ Determine who can approve budgets, make changes to the acceptance criteria, and modify requirements.

  ○ Agree on how to measure the project customer's level of satisfaction with the final deliverable.

  ○ Note: If criteria are not yet available, refer to the document or standard that will detail the criteria, such as a test plan, specification, or published industry standards, etc.

Project Scope Overview

Project name: *3-Day conference on project management*

Customers' requirements:

1. *There should be a blend of general-interest and special-interest sessions.*

2. *At least 2 hours per day should be factored in for networking opportunities.*

Final Deliverable
3-Day conference on project management

8. Describe the organizational deliverables.

- An *organizational deliverable* is a product, service, process, or result that is created to meet an organizational need or requirement (not a customer requirement).

- An organizational deliverable may be a by-product of creating the final deliverable or may be an additional deliverable.

- Example: a report on a new area of technology that a team uses in producing a final deliverable for a customer. This report is for the organization and was created to complete the project.

- Do not include deliverables that you will create for an outside customer (see step 6).

CASE STUDY

Organizational Deliverables for the 3-Day Conference

Organizational Deliverable: *"Project Management Process Report"*

The team members of the 3-day conference project will use the project management process that the organization has recently adopted and summarize their experience in the report.

9. Define the acceptance criteria for any organizational deliverables.
   - If the sponsor doesn't define these criteria, develop proposed criteria and give to the sponsor for approval.
10. Identify the project's major stakeholders.
    - *Stakeholders* are people or groups that will be affected by and care about the project.
    - They have formal or informal authority over the impacted groups and can affect the success of the project.
    - They usually do not have approval authority (unless they are also on the project team), but if they support the project, it will be easier.
    - They may be able to influence the project sponsor or customer.
    - Stakeholders are not members of the project team.

Complete the Project Assurance Section of the Project Charter

The purpose of the project assurance section is to set the tone for managing the risk on the project.

Why do it?

To define the maximum degree of risk that is allowed on the project. These *risk limits* help the team develop corrective or preventive measures for any unacceptable level of risk. To define the required approvals, *status reports*, and other communications requested by management, usually for oversight.

How do I do it?

1. Establish the tolerance for risk—risk limits—for the project.

   ○ The _risk limit_ is the amount of risk the organization is willing to accept on the project. It is a strategic choice.

   ○ When you later prepare the project management plan, you will analyze the project's risk level and compare the risk limit to the project's risk level.

   ○ Using a scale from 1 to 10, assign a number to represent the risk limit for the project. (If you prefer, use "high," "medium," and "low.")

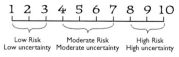

   ○ Where possible, explain which types of risk are acceptable and which are not, or quantify unacceptable consequences in financial costs, delays, or quality.

2. Identify critical or mandatory reviews and approvals.

   ○ Identify checkpoints (also known as tollgates or sign-offs) for assuring quality on the project.

   ○ Define the reviews and approvals requested by the project customer or sponsor. Note the _reason_ for each review or approval.

   ○ Include the project customer in this process, where appropriate.

People often want to be part of the review and approval process. Evaluate each such request to make sure it will add value.

During planning, team members will create their own list of reviews when they write the project management plan. This portion of the project charter should focus on describing reviews required by the organization and project customers.

3. Describe the communications—that is, status reports—that the organization requires at a high level.

   ○ Status reports are used by management to monitor the project. The sponsor should specify his needs from these reports. If he doesn't, the team will describe planned communications in the project management plan.

   ○ Specify the frequency and content of each report.

Complete the Resources Section of the Project Charter

Why do it?

To communicate the resource limits—human, schedule, and monetary—that are available or allocated for the project.

When the project was selected, a cost–benefit analysis or return on investment (ROI) may have been performed, and these limits may represent the investment the organization is willing to make based on the expected benefits.

How do I do it?

1. Choose the project manager and initial team members.

   ○ Assign a project manager—someone who is skilled in leadership, facilitation, coordination of tasks, communication, and project management knowledge.

   ○ For some projects, at this point it is obvious who (or what functions) are needed on the project team. If so, list them if appropriate.

- Optional: list the names of the individuals or groups that are assigned to the project team.
- Look for the right blend of skills, influence, and knowledge.

CASE STUDY

Selecting the Initial Team for the 3-Day Conference

Representatives have been selected to be on the team and will lead subproject teams within their own work from these areas. They will be subproject leaders.

Project Team	Work Area
Jose Ferrara	Facilities
Andy Wellman	Marketing
Ralph Panetta	Print Shop
Linda Saunders	Member Services
Amy Lee (Project Leader)	Project Management

 Consider including the project customer or possibly a key supplier on the project team.

2. Determine the project's deadlines.
- List the dates that *must* be met, including completion of the final deliverable. These are the *deadlines*.
- During development of the project charter, you only need to know the deadlines. The important dates for completion of the project will be determined and approved during planning (see Chapter 4).
- Avoid giving unnecessary deadlines. It's the team's job—and not the project sponsor's—to plan how best to reach the real deadlines on the project.

The Project Management Memory Jogger™ 2nd edition | ©2010 GOAL/QPC

○ Don't forget to set deadlines for any organizational deliverables that are required for your project. For example, the sponsor of the 3-day conference wants the "Project Management Process Report" issued by December 31.

Deadline For the Final Deliverable
The 3-day conference will be held on September 27, 28, and 29.

Additional Deadlines for the 3-Day Conference

Conference Plan	*August 1*
Project Management Process Report	*Dec 31*

3. Determine the limits on effort.

○ External staffing costs (contractors, etc.) may or may not be included in this limit. You should verify these limits with the project sponsor.

○ The effort limit is the maximum amount of effort allowed on the project.

○ One way to state the maximum effort is in terms of the number of hours or FTEs (full-time equivalents). Example: If you are limiting the effort to three people working half-time, that would equal to 1.5 FTEs working on the project.

○ Other alternatives: "no more than 20 percent of your time"; "one day every two weeks for three months"; "one two-hour meeting once a week."

The project team may not be aware of, or involved in, the decision to initiate the project. Give the reasons for the limit, such as the importance of the project or its value to the organization or project customer.

 Effort limits are usually based on calculations of the project's return on investment or a cost-benefit analysis.

4. Determine the project's cost objective/spending limit.

   ○ This is the maximum amount of money authorized for the project.

   ○ Tell the team what is included in the limit: internal costs (effort, supplies, copies, equipment) and external costs (contract labor, materials, travel, training, etc.).

 Be realistic about limits on effort and spending. Allow adequate resources to complete the project.

5. List any organizational constraints on the project.

   ○ These are the constraints—other than deadlines and cost limits—that the project must conform to.

   ○ Use only those project constraints that are essential. The project team should have the freedom to determine how to complete the project, as long as project objectives are met.

CASE STUDY

Constraints on the 3-Day Conference

1. *No additional staff can be hired.*
2. *No capital equipment purchases.*
3. *Only audiovisual services can be outsourced.*

Review, Approve, and Distribute the Project Charter

Why do it?

To ensure approval of the project charter and to communicate information to stakeholders. The project charter sets the requirements and the limits for the project and forms the basis for creating a detailed plan.

 Include any information in the charter that would be useful to the team. The more direction up front, the less time it will take to complete a project plan that is in line with the needs and expectations of the organization and project customers.

How do I do it?

1. Before the project charter is submitted to the project sponsor and customer for approval, review the charter with the project manager and team for feedback.

2. Obtain approval of the project charter.

   ○ If the project sponsor completed the charter, review with the project manager and team for comments, questions, and understanding.

   ○ If the project team completed the project charter, the project manager should review it with the project sponsor and customer, modify as needed, and obtain sponsor approval.

3. Issue the project charter.

   ○ Distribute copies of the project charter to . . .

      ○ Project sponsor
      ○ All members of the project team
      ○ Functional managers who will be affected by the project
      ○ The customer, where appropriate
      ○ The project steering group or project office, if applicable
      ○ Major stakeholders

Project Charter

Prepared by: Chris Wheeler, Sponsor
and Amy Lee, Project Manager

Date issued: January 7

Project name: 3-Day Conference on Project Management [step 1]

PROJECT SCOPE

Business Problem/Opportunity [step 2]
[Reason for the project]
Project managers, team members, sponsors, project customers, functional managers, and others who work on projects need a better understanding of their roles on projects and current best practices.

Operational Results
[The expected impact on the business; may be aspirational or numerical goal]

1. Attendees will improve their skills to better manage projects.

2. Attendees will make contacts with people who are practicing project management to share best practices.

Project Customer(s) [step 3]
[Name of person]

Chris Wheeler (also the project sponsor)

(Note: The conference attendees are the users of the conference, represented by Chris Wheeler.)

Project Decision Criteria
[Faster, better, or cheaper] [step 4]

1. Lower cost.
2. More features.
3. Since the conference dates are fixed, earlier delivery is not an option.

Customer Requirements
[Features and functions of the final deliverable] [step 5]

- There should be a blend of general-interest and special-interest sessions.
- At least 2 hours per day should be factored in for networking opportunities.

Final Deliverable(s)

[Product, process, service, result] [step 6]

A 3-day conference on project management

Final Deliverable Acceptance Criteria

[Scope objective] [step 7]

Evaluations = rating of at least 4 out of 5 by attendees

Organizational Deliverable(s)

[Product, service, process, result] [step 8]

"Project Management Process Report"

Organizational Deliverable Acceptance Criteria

[step 9]

Report to be issued in accordance with company standard procedure #xxx.

Major Stakeholders

[Groups, departments] [step 10]

- Project managers of the organization
- Project sponsors of the organization

PROJECT ASSURANCE

Project Risk Limit

[Tolerance for risk] [step 1]

- 3-day project management conference: limit of 2 (or low)
- Project Management Process Report: limit of 2 (or low)

Reviews & Approvals [step 2]

- Final program: sponsor
- Hotel contract: sponsor

Reports Required [step 3]

Weekly project status report

PROJECT RESOURCES

Team Assignments

[Names or groups] [step 1]

Project Manager: Amy Lee (Project Manager)

Project Team: Jose Ferrera (Facilities)

Andy Wellman (Marketing)

Ralph Panetta (Print Shop)

Linda Saunders (Member Services)

Deadlines

[Schedule objective] [step 2]

- Conference September 27–29
- Conference plan August 1
- "Project Management Process Report" December 31

Effort Limit

[Maximum number of hours or FTEs] [step 3]

None. The team should estimate the time required and then monitor the actual hours invested.

Spending Limit

[Cost objective] [step 4]

External costs $90,000

Organizational Constraints

[Required to do or not do] [step 5]

1. No additional staff can be hired.
2. No capital equipment can be purchased.
3. Only audiovisual services can be outsourced.

Chapter

THREE

HOW TO WORK TOGETHER AS A TEAM

At the project kickoff meeting, the project team will benefit greatly if the members agree on a basic set of ground rules for participating on the project team, running meetings, and resolving conflicts. Many items need follow-up after meetings, so keeping track of these issues is essential. And holding virtual team meetings (teleconferences, webinars, and videoconferences) presents its own set of issues that require skillful handling.

For more details on this topic, see *The Advanced Project Management Memory Jogger™*

When you need to:	Do this activity:	Page #
Agree on a basic set of team ground rules	Develop Ground Rules	39
Capture meeting ideas that you want to follow up but are off topic at the moment	Create a Parking Lot	45
Monitor and control the resolution of issues (open action items) that remain unresolved at the end of a project meeting	Create an Issues List	47
Improve your meetings	Evaluate Your Meetings	49
Get the most out of telephone and teleconference meetings	Hold Effective Virtual Team Meetings	53
Gain the cooperation of project team members	Adopt Effective Leadership Techniques	58

Develop Ground Rules

Ground rules are principles that each project team member agrees to follow in project team meetings.

Why do it?

To keep project meetings on track, define expectations for team members' behavior, and document the principles that the team supports. Having ground rules helps reduce stress and makes it easier to resolve problems when they arise.

Keep written documentation of key decisions and agreements in all meetings. These meeting notes should include, at minimum, the agenda and the results of each agenda item and issues list.

 If your team protests, ask, "Could our meetings be more pleasant and efficient? Would you like to have better meetings? Would that help the project?"

How do I do it?

1. In the first meeting of team members, have the members brainstorm typical meeting problems.

   ○ After brainstorming these problems, the team can discuss them and choose which, if any, they want to resolve.

Brainstorming Tips

When you need to generate ideas for discussion and problem solving in a quick and efficient way, **Write it, Say it, Slap it**™ is a versatile and effective tool. Use it for these kinds of tasks:

o Assessing project risk

o Creating team ground rules

o Identifying customers, specifying customer requirements, and determining interim deliverables

o Finding solutions to problems, dealing with issues, accommodating project changes, responding to risks, and exploiting opportunities

Write it, Say it, Slap it is a great method to use whenever the team finds itself mired down and needs to refocus.

Here's how it works.

1. Determine the issue or topic.

2. Give each team member a marker pen and a pad of 3×3 sticky notes.

3. Start brainstorming to generate ideas.

   - Team members *write* their ideas on sticky notes—one idea per note.
   - They *say it* out loud.
   - They *slap* the note on a piece of flip chart paper.

4. Process the ideas. Discuss, clarify, understand, explain, carefully evaluate duplicates, if any, and group or decide as appropriate.

When you're brainstorming, keep these tips in mind.

   - Don't think, censor, or judge ideas.
   - All ideas are good ideas.
   - Don't discuss the ideas during brainstorming. You will process them later.
   - Duplicate ideas are OK. Don't stop if you hear someone say what you are writing. It probably isn't the same.
   - Say, "We only have two minutes" (more or less—it's up to you).
   - Or say, "Our stretch goal for the number of ideas is at least eight per person" or as many as you think will move things along.
   - Brainstorm as many ideas as possible.

Brainstorming Tips for Virtual Teams

The project manager leads the team through the steps.

For a teleconference . . .

o Select a note taker or use Instant Messaging (IM) to collect and publish the results.

o Each person uses Write it, Say it, Slap it at the same time at her desk or in a meeting room. (The synergy and energy of the team and the piggyback opportunity outweigh the chaos.)

o Get all the people from one location in the same room.

For a webinar . . .

o Determine who will collect and publish the results.

o Use the whiteboard webinar feature or the IM chat feature.

o To avoid writing on top of each other's words, designate the quadrants of the whiteboard space. On the next page is an example.

Example of assigned spaces for using a white board or a webinar

Chris, Catie	Theresa, John
Jamal, Devon	Lee, Julia

Divide the space into quadrants, and assign one-fourth of the participants to each section.

2. Develop ground rules to minimize or prevent the problems.
   - Use the problems identified in step 1 to decide what to include in the ground rules.
   - For examples, see "All About Ground Rules," page 44.

 You can use Write it, Say it, Slap it to develop responses to these problems.

3. Review the ground rules at the beginning of each meeting, whether virtual or in person.

All About Ground Rules

Remember these criteria for good ground rules:
- They are simple, brief, and clear.
- They address problems that often arise in meetings.
- They minimize confusion, disruptions, and conflicts.
- They improve the project team's effectiveness and efficiency.
- They are general guidelines and not rigid laws.
- They are achievable and realistic and are revised as needed.

Here are some sample ground rules:
- One person speaks at a time.
- Listen and show respect.
- Use computers, cell/smart phones only *outside* the meeting room or during breaks. Using these devices in the meeting is distracting for those around you even though you may think you can multitask and still participate in the meeting.
- No side conversations.
- Have an agenda, and stick to it.
- Use the parking lot and issues list (discussed later in this chapter).

When someone breaks the ground rules in a meeting, here are some possible responses.
- Decide whether it's a problem.
- Consider giving feedback, either on the spot or later, in private.
- Discuss the issue as a team.
- If appropriate, change the ground rule.

Create a Parking Lot

A *parking lot* is a place to capture ideas that the team doesn't want to lose but are not appropriate to the discussion at hand.

CASE STUDY

Do we need a marketing plan?

What is the printer deadline?

Do we have the right software?

Who can write the copy?

Why do it?

To keep meetings focused (to resist being sidetracked or to avoid distractions) but honor the ideas, questions, and concerns of those present as they arise. A parking lot allows the team to move on when an issue does not involve the whole team or is a lower priority and can be handled later. Placing items in the parking lot lets you acknowledge the contributions of individuals and help team members feel that what they say or think matters.

How do I do it?

During a meeting—whether in person or virtual—team members may have questions, concerns, or comments that are not relevant to the item being discussed. When that happens, follow these steps.

1. Ask the person with the question to write the idea on a sticky note in her own words.

2. Place the note on a flip chart or other suitable place with the other notes. This is your parking lot.

   ○ The meeting leader then continues with the original agenda item, uninterrupted.

3. At the end of the meeting, review the items in the parking lot.

   ○ Quickly process the sticky notes.

   ○ Typically, most of the items will have been addressed.

   ○ Any that were covered in the meeting need no additional action.

   ○ Some can be resolved now if time permits. Record any decisions in the meeting notes or minutes, and include them in the project status report(s) as appropriate.

   ○ Assign the remaining items to the relevant team members: send the items to the issues list (discussed next), where they will stay until resolved.

 If the issue or concern is beyond the project team's authority, scope, or purview, put it on the issues list for future resolution, and forward it to the appropriate individual, usually the project sponsor.

 Be sure to save time for clearing the parking lot at the end of the meeting.

Handling the Parking Lot When Your Meetings Are Virtual

On the phone . . .
Assign one person to record parking lot issues as they arise. Read them back to the team at the end of the meeting, and process them.

On a webinar . . .
Use instant messaging or the chat feature to record the ideas, or use a whiteboard space as your parking lot.

Create an Issues List

In project meetings, team members often raise important issues that need action but can't or shouldn't be resolved during the meeting. These issues represent decisions or answers that team members need if they're to proceed with project work. Such issues may be internal or external to the team. Project teams can use an *issues list* to manage these issues.

The issues list is *not* a to-do list or a substitute for a schedule.

Why do it?

To monitor and control the resolution of issues (open action items) that remain unresolved at the end of each project meeting.

If it's unclear whether an item belongs on the issues list, write it on a sticky note and save it in the parking lot. At the end of the meeting, review it to decide whether it's an item that belongs on the issues list.

How do I do it?

1. Create a spreadsheet or database for recording the issues. Design it to include . . .

   - An identifying number for each issue
   - A description of the issue
   - The person who wants the issue resolved
   - The person or group responsible for resolving issues
   - The deadline for resolution
   - The date when it was resolved
   - The way it was resolved

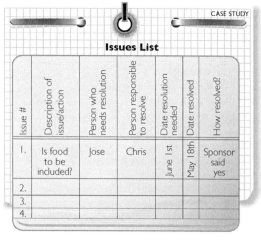

CASE STUDY

Issues List

Issue #	Description of issue/action	Person who needs resolution	Person responsible to resolve	Date resolution needed	Date resolved	How resolved?
1.	Is food to be included?	Jose	Chris	June 1st	May 18th	Sponsor said yes
2.						
3.						
4.						

To reduce rework, when you add items to the issues list be sure to include the information needed to resolve the issue.

2. Review the issues list at team meetings.
   - When an issue is resolved, record the date and describe how it was resolved.
   - Prioritize open issues by due date and importance.

 The project manager is responsible for making sure that all issues are recorded, tracked, and resolved on time.

3. Include the issues list in the project meeting notes.
   - Add "issues list review and update" to the meeting agenda. Add any new issues, and close resolved ones.

 Recording how the issue was resolved can be a valuable source of lessons learned at the end of the project during closeout. Resolving every issue takes time and energy, and it may require rework. Understanding the reasons for the issue can lead to greater efficiencies in the next project.

Evaluate Your Meetings

At the end of each meeting, project teams should take a few minutes to evaluate the meeting itself and assess how well their meeting process is working.

Why do it?

To make small course corrections at each meeting to improve the quality of your meetings and the efficiency and effectiveness of your meeting process. Frequent, small pieces of feedback allow the team to continuously improve the quality of meetings in a way that is quick, nonthreatening, and easy. People feel heard, and you have the opportunity to make small adjustments to resolve small problems before they become big resentments. When done regularly, this kind of review also raises team members' awareness of team dynamics, improving self-awareness and social interaction.

How do I do it?

1. Prepare the team for a meeting evaluation by asking . . .

   ○ What parts of the meeting worked well ("Do again")?

   ○ What can we do differently next time ("Do differently")?

   ○ On a scale of 1 to 10, how did we do ("Score")?

2. At the end of the meeting, ask team members to say . . .

   ○ One thing we should do again next time

   ○ One thing we should do differently next time

   ○ How they would score the meeting (10 *is excellent*)

 For these comments, allow 30 seconds maximum per person. For a 10-person meeting, it takes only 5 minutes. If the team is engaged and wants to spend more time discussing these issues in a productive way, consider allowing more time.

3. Record and discuss the results on the following form on a flip chart or whiteboard, where everyone can see, and include them in the meeting notes or status report.

○ Include items that cover start and end times, pace, quality of discussion, and so on.

Use webinar or teleconference techniques to review and record the results.

Example of Meeting Evaluation			
Person	Do again	Do differently	#
Julia	Started on time	Have all the groups represented	7
Ava	Good discussion	Follow agenda	8
Jordan	Resolved issues	Provide agenda in advance	9
		Total Score	24
		Average	8

4. Average the scores.

○ Consider including the scores in the meeting notes.

○ Track the scores over time to see progress.

○ Ask, "What would the perfect meeting be like?" Note trends and large variations in ratings among individuals.

What would you do as project manager if your team evaluation scored the meeting with wide differences in perception, such as a 1 and a 10 in the same meeting? Would this information be useful in leading your team?

Processing Meeting Evaluation Comments

Some teams gather feedback on their process and then file it away without processing it. That's a waste of everyone's time. Instead, use the evaluations to make a real difference in your meetings. Here are ideas to process the comments in the meeting.

- Put the feedback on the issues list.
- If time permits, discuss it in the meeting.
- If a specific team member seems to be the issue, schedule a private meeting between the person and the project manager.
- Assign one or more team members to take the comment and come back with recommendations.

If the project manager does not address these comments and allow healthy discussion, then the team will not feel that the process works. People may lose interest and stop their efforts to improve.

Here are ideas for processing the comments outside the meeting:

- Discuss the issue with the project sponsor, as appropriate.
- Get coaching.
- Ask others how they handled it.
- Get a facilitator.

Hold Effective Virtual Team Meetings

Virtual teams usually meet via telephone, teleconference, or Web-based applications, which typically do not allow team members to see each other.

 It generally takes more time to hold a meeting in a virtual setting than in person. To save time, when you're taking roll, evaluating the meeting, or polling, call on participants—it's faster. Some hesitate, others dominate. Post the order of speakers so that participants will be prepared to respond.

Why do it?

In organizations where the team comes from different locations, virtual team meetings are often the only option available. Unfortunately, telephone or teleconference meetings are less effective than face-to-face meetings. The participants, sitting at their desks, are likely to multitask, diminishing their ability to pay attention. In addition, people often don't get the full meaning of the message because they can't see others' body language and facial expressions.

Project teams can take specific steps to make virtual meetings as effective as possible.

How do I do it?

1. Prepare for the meeting.
   - In the meeting invitation, clearly state the time of the meeting; use Greenwich Mean Time (GMT).
   - Distribute handouts, including an agenda, well in advance of the meeting, and use version control.
   - Choose variable times for meetings so that the same people aren't inconvenienced every time due to differences in time zones.

Tip Consider offering a brief bio of each project team member, including her role on the project, at the first meeting. Include a photo to put a face and background with each voice.

- ○ Learn and use conference call or Web meeting management features, such as the mute feature.
- ○ Distribute the ground rules, and review them at the beginning of the meeting.

2. During the meeting, observe special guidelines.
   - ○ Start on time. Call any missing participants, in case they forgot about the meeting. It happens.
   - ○ Speak loudly and clearly into the phone. Be aware of background noise.
   - ○ Place any nonproject business issues in the parking lot, and cover them last so that those who are not involved can leave the call.
   - ○ Begin a question with the name of the person it is directed to.
   - ○ When you refer to the handouts, cite specifics, such as page or paragraph number. (Paragraph numbers are helpful.)

3. Observe phone etiquette tips.
   - ○ Identify yourself before speaking.
   - ○ Announce your presence in the call when you enter and when you exit.
   - ○ Put the phone on mute when you are not speaking. This practice minimizes keyboard and other background noises and does not activate hold music.

4. At the end of the meeting, take steps to close the meeting and improve your meeting process.
   - ○ Summarize results and agreements
   - ○ Decide how the meeting notes or status report will be distributed.
   - ○ Thank everyone for participating.
   - ○ Use a few minutes to evaluate the meeting (see "Evaluate Your Meetings" earlier in the chapter).

Organizing Team Files and E-mail

Some project teams have access to cloud-based online collaboration tools to assist in organizing e-mail and files. For those teams that do not have or use these tools, and to help team members deal with overflowing inboxes, agree on the format of the e-mail subject line. In this way, team members can glean key information at a glance before they open the message.

Here's how it works:

ProjectName/Topic/Action/ResponsiblePerson/ Completion Date/Urgency

- ○ Project Name: Keep it short; use a code or acronym.
- ○ Topic: The subject of the e-mail. Again, keep it short—perhaps key words or the name of the subproject.
- ○ Action: What you want the recipient to do—for example, FYI, decision, action.

ABC/Safety/Decision/Yvonne/28Feb/Urgent

- Responsible Person: The name or initials of the person.
- Completion Date: The due date for any needed action. Use day/month.
- Urgency: If the action is urgent, put that at the end.

In the following illustration, you can easily see that the sender urgently needs a decision from the recipient by February 28 regarding safety in the ABC project.

If you're sending a message to multiple people for different actions, you can use this format:
ABC/Safety/FYI: Robin/Action: Stacey

If you follow this convention, you can sort your e-mail by project, and all e-mail on a given topic will be together.

For file names, design a similar naming convention that fits your project. Put the date or version of the document in the file name so that people can determine whether they are looking at the correct or latest version. Be disciplined in using your chosen protocol. If used correctly, it can really help.

Using Consensus-Based Decision-Making Tools

When people participate in discussions and decisions, they contribute information and insight to the process, resulting in better decisions. Many projects are on a tight schedule, and often people think they don't have time to develop consensus. It is unrealistic to always get unanimous agreement, and it's unnecessary if you can get *consensus*—a general agreement among the members of the project team to support a given decision or approach.

Consensus-Based Team Decision-Making Tools

When you need to:	Do this activity:	Page #
Develop a list of key issues from many differing viewpoints—for example, identifying the reasons for poor team performance	Affinity Diagram	194
Identify, analyze, and classify key issues to find the root cause or main driver —for example, finding the factor that has the most impact on success	Interrelationship Digraph	205
Choose the best option when there are multiple weighted criteria or closely related options—for example, choosing the best person to lead the project	Prioritization Matrices	216

Adopt Effective Leadership Techniques

Why do it?

To develop strong interpersonal and social skills for using persuasion, influence, logic, and data to lead project team members. In many projects the project manager does not have direct authority over the project team members, so he needs interpersonal skills and influence skills to gain their cooperation.

 The Advanced Project Management Memory Jogger™ addresses project leadership issues.

When you need to ...	Check this section in *The Advanced Project Memory Jogger™*
Work on team communication	Chapter 8
Handle negotiation and conflict	Chapter 9
Improve your leadership and understand emotional intelligence	Chapter 10

How do I do it?

1. Keep the project team on track.
   - Set a time limit for the topic.
   - Take a break.
   - Table the topic: use the issues list or the parking lot.
   - Ask for ideas and input from the group: "How can we solve our problem?"

 Remember that as project manager, you have options for running better meetings and stopping disruptive behavior. Your goal is to redirect team members' energy when things aren't going well.

2. Deal effectively with people problems.
   - Use constructive feedback (usually one-on-one) to discuss the problem with the person.
   - Ask a non-participating team member to lead the discussion or take notes.
   - Interrupt, if needed.
   - End the meeting, if the problem is severe.
   - Call out or confront incorrect information.
   - Make eye contact, and then pause.

3. Help the team when it is mired down.
   - Refocus the group on the agenda.
   - Use brainstorming or decision-making tools.
   - Break the team into smaller groups to work on solutions.
   - Revise the agenda during the meeting if appropriate.

Before choosing a response, consider the risks and benefits. Match your response to the situation and your desired outcome or goal. Ask yourself three questions:

Will it help?

What are the consequences?

Will it work?

4. Work to develop your project team culture.

- ○ Use the ground rules to capture what the team cares about.
- ○ Define things such as "on time" so that the team is working from the same understanding.
- ○ Conduct and use meeting evaluations.
- ○ Treat all people and ideas with respect.

Dealing with Cross-Cultural Project Teams

Project team members come to the table with many kinds of differences: generational, geographic, religious, socioeconomic, and so on. People also come from different industries and different departments, and they have different attitudes and thinking styles. Although these differences can be sources of conflict, they also can enrich your project team if you manage them appropriately.

Here are some team tips:

- Set goals to be aware, polite, and respectful. Consider adding these to the ground rules.
- Listen, ask questions, and recognize everyone.
- Don't use jargon that your listeners don't understand. For example, don't use technical engineering terms when you're speaking to non-engineers.
- Be careful when you're using English expressions. You may know what I mean when I say a project "crashed and burned" or when you refer to a project as a "death march," but these expressions may baffle people who speak English as a second language.
- Empathize, be sincere, be caring, and don't judge.

Acknowledge that there are too many world cultures for you to be an expert on each one or even to be aware of all the cultural issues. Use these tips to help you and the team navigate the cross-cultural landscape.

 Often, the best common ground among project team members is the larger company culture. When cultural differences present a problem, emphasize company policies and strategies.

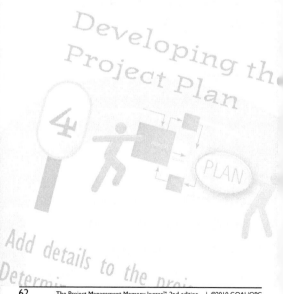

Developing the
Project Plan

4

PLAN

Add details to the proj
Determin

Chapter

FOUR

HOW TO CREATE THE PROJECT MANAGEMENT PLAN

A *project management plan* is written by the project manager and the project team, and it is approved by the project sponsor. The plan describes what the team plans to produce (the interim and final deliverables), the risks to the project, the project schedules, the resources needed to complete the project, and so on. To successfully execute a project, the project team must first create a good project management plan.

The overview chart on the next page shows fourteen broad categories of the typical activities you'll need to consider when you create your project management plan. This chapter explains each of these activities in detail.

Which specific activities will your team need to work on? That depends on whether your project is simple or complex. Complex projects usually require all these planning activities. To determine whether to do an activity, review the "When you need to" columns in the charts and the "Why do it?" statements for each activity. If you understand these activities, you will be better positioned to make the right choices in planning your project.

When you need to:	Do this activity:	Page #
Specify the interim and final deliverables	Define the Project Scope	66
Determine if there are potential risks to the project and develop responses	Analyze the Project Risks	82
Improve project outcomes	Prepare a Project Quality Plan	90
Ensure that project materials, equipment, etc., are available when needed	Prepare a Project Procurement Plan	92
Ask whether the right people have been included on the team	Review Team Membership	96
Develop schedules for completing the project	Create a Project Schedule	101
Estimate the effort, time, or money you need to set aside for unforeseen problems	Calculate the Project's Contingency	114

When you need to:	Do this activity:	Page #
Estimate how much staff time will be needed to do the project	Estimate the Effort Required for the Project	119
Estimate how much money will be required to do the project	Create a Project Budget	127
Plan key communications to be transmitted during the project	Create a Communication Plan	133
Plan for rollout and implementation of new or improved deliverables	Deal with Organizational Change	137
Assemble the project management plan and obtain approval	Assemble the Project Management Plan	141
Define the stages of development of the deliverables	Deliverable Life Cycle Stages	177
Determine when each activity needs to be completed and by whom	Activity Schedule	183

Define the Project Scope

The purpose of your project is to create a unique product, service, process, or result (deliverables) that will satisfy the project customer. The *project scope* identifies and defines the project customers, the final deliverables, and the acceptance criteria that the customers will use to measure satisfaction with the final deliverables.

When you need to:	Do this activity:	Page #
Make sure everyone understands what the project will produce	Develop the Project Scope Description and Acceptance Criteria	67
Break down the final deliverables into smaller, more manageable pieces.	Determine the Interim Deliverables for the Project	72
Know where the team's responsibility for the project begins and ends.	Analyze the Project Boundaries	74
Identify subprojects and work assignments for each team member.	Create a Work Breakdown Structure (WBS) of Subprojects and Work Assignments	78

Customer acceptance criteria should be SMART: specific, measurable, achievable, realistic, and tangible. See step 4 on page 71

SMART Acceptance Criteria

S	Specific	• Can be understood only one way • Free of ambiguities and unverifiable terms • Stated positively
M	Measurable	• Can be verified
A	Achievable	• Can be done within project constraints
R	Realistic	• Makes sense • Is appropriate for the requirement
T	Tangible	• Stated in numerical form or yes/no format, or in accordance with an established, understood, and recognized definition, procedure, or standard

The Advanced Project Management Memory Jogger™

Develop the Project Scope Description and Acceptance Criteria

Why do it?

To make sure there is agreement between the project team, project sponsor, and project customer on what the project will deliver.

How do I do it?

1. Review the project scope section of the project charter, and make sure everyone on the team understands it

   ○ This section of the project charter defines the following information:

- Business problem or opportunity
- Project customer and key stakeholders
- Customer requirements and priorities
- Final and organizational deliverables
- Deliverables' acceptance criteria
- If the team members do not understand the scope of the project as described in the project charter, ask the project sponsor for clarification before moving on.

2. If there is more than one customer, create a customer table to identify the customer roles and the authority each one has.

- Determine who can approve budgets, make changes in acceptance criteria, and modify requirements. In complex projects, there may be multiple customers; be sure to clarify exactly which function or area each one controls.

A customer table can help you capture this information. To start, have the team members brainstorm all of the project's customers and stakeholders, then list their requirements.

- Not all projects need a customer table and some projects may have more customers than the three basic ones listed in the example below. If you have multiple customers and conflicting requirements, you will need to convene a meeting to resolve any differences.

- The project sponsor can help facilitate mutual agreement.

Customer Table			
Customer or Functional Role*	Asks the Question:	Customer Role Approves or Disapproves:	Accountable Individual
Economic or financial	Is it worth the investment	Expenditures	(Name of authorizing individual)
Technical	Does it meet the technical specifications? Will it work?	Technical issues	(Name of authorizing individual)
User	Will it do what I need it to do?	Functionality or user interface	(Name of authorizing individual)

* One person may fill one or more of these roles, and you may have additional roles. The Advanced Project Management Memory Jogger™

3. Create a deliverables table to list and describe the final deliverables.

- ○ The *deliverables table* summarizes the project's deliverables and provides high-level information about requirements and acceptance criteria.

- ○ The project charter identifies the project's final deliverables but typically not in very much detail. In a document to accompany the deliverables table, write a description of each deliverable in as much detail as needed for the project sponsor and project customers to have a clear and complete understanding of what will be produced.

- ○ To produce the best option for the project customer and end user, be sure you understand the business problem or opportunity that the deliverable fulfills.

Deliverables Table

Deliverables	Description	Type of Authorization	Customer Requirements (Features and Functions)	Customer Acceptance Criteria
Name of deliverable	Briefly describe narrative	Name of the person who represents users and has authority to approve the deliverable	What the customer has asked for	Customer's criteria for acceptance
Deliverable 1				
Deliverable 2				
Deliverable n				

The Advanced Project Management Memory Jogger™

○ Organizational deliverables, if applicable, can be listed in this table.

Use clear, plain language in the deliverables table. Misunderstandings and miscommunication are the source of as many as 75% of project problems.

Write exactly what you will produce, succinctly. Avoid using industry jargon or acronyms.

4. Define the customer's criteria for accepting the final deliverables.

○ Recall that *acceptance criteria* are the measurements the customer will use to accept or reject the final deliverable.

○ Review the customer's acceptance criteria as defined in the project charter.

○ Ask the customer whether the list is complete, and add criteria as needed.

○ Make the criteria SMART: specific, measurable, achievable, realistic, and tangible.

If you don't have all the information you need to apply each of the SMART standards, then either stop to collect the information, put it on the issues list, or determine whether the standard is necessary for success.

Be sure to involve the project customers as well as the project team in this effort. You'll get more accurate information and better buy-in for the project.

For a detailed analysis of project requirements, particularly in IT, see *The Software Requirements Memory Jogger™*.

Determine the Interim Deliverables for the Project

Why do it?

To describe the *interim deliverables*: those that the team must produce during the project before it can complete the final deliverable. Completion of the major interim deliverables usually coincides with the project's milestones.

 A *milestone* is a significant point or event in the project, usually a major achievement or accomplishment.

How do I do it?

1. Define the interim deliverables that you will produce for each final deliverable.

   ○ Final deliverables, whether for the project or any subprojects, have interim deliverables. Interim deliverables are used to build the work breakdown structure later in this chapter ("Create a Work Breakdown Structure (WBS)."

 In our sample project, the conference guide is a subproject final deliverable, and the list of speakers is an interim deliverable.

   ○ If you know how to proceed, or if the deliverable is familiar to the team, try one or more of the following:

- To generate the list of interim deliverables, think chronologically. What will the team produce first? What should be produced after that? Continue listing interim deliverables until you get to the final deliverable.
- Use templates, or refer to previous similar projects.

- If you aren't sure how to proceed or if the deliverable is not familiar to the team, try one or more of the following:

  - Brainstorm the deliverables using Write it, Say it, Slap it (see Chapter 3).
  - Alternatively, you can start with the final deliverable and work backward, asking, "What would we need to have in order to create this deliverable?" In other words, base each deliverable on the previous (predecessor) deliverable.

2. Organize the interim deliverables you have defined.

  - Select the main interim deliverables (the ones that would be at the highest level of an outline); seven to ten is a good target number. If you have more than that, choose only the most important ones.
  - Put the chosen interim deliverables into chronological order (but do not assign dates yet). Make sure that you've accounted for all the most important interim deliverables.

Save the list of deliverables that were not chosen in this step, because they can be useful later for detailed planning.

3. If the quality of an interim deliverable could have a significant impact on the quality of a final deliverable, define the acceptance criteria for that interim deliverable.

○ Some but not all of the interim deliverables may need acceptance criteria.

○ Monitoring the quality of interim deliverables helps ensure that each final deliverable will meet the customer's acceptance criteria.

○ Make the criteria SMART (see page 67).

 Using SMART criteria is especially useful when the deliverable is new, one you haven't made before, is being created by a supplier you haven't used before, and so on.

 It's easier to address quality issues as the project moves along than to wait until the final deliverable is complete. That's why it's important to define acceptance criteria for certain interim deliverables.

 When it's warranted, identify checkpoints or tollgates as the deliverable progresses.

Analyze the Project Boundaries

Why do it?

To identify where the team's responsibilities for the project start and end. Projects tend to interact and overlap with other activities in an organization. The team members need to know which activities are included in the project scope—and which are excluded. In this way, they can coordinate their project work with stakeholder groups and with work in other projects or departments.

How do I do it?

1. Identify the items and areas that are and are not part of the project scope.

   ○ Brainstorm areas that are *in scope* (things the team is accountable to produce) and *out of scope* (things the team is not accountable to produce).

 For brainstorming tips, see Chapter 3.

CASE STUDY

3-Day Conference

The items that are part of the project scope are:

- *Contracting and facilities set-up*

- *Marketing*

- *Graphic design and printing*

- *Registration*

- *Program development*

2. Identify any stakeholders, groups, or functional areas that will significantly affect (*or be affected by*) the project.

   ○ Brainstorm inputs and outputs to the project.

   ○ Review the deliverables.

   ○ Ask the project sponsor and customer for ideas.

3-Day Conference

The project that is affected by the 3-day conference, but is not part of the project scope, is the:

- *Billing process improvement project affects the 3-Day Conference project because the registration fees and travel expenses of the participants will be internally cross-charged to the various internal departments. The timing of that project may affect internal billing and the accounting codes to be used.*

also keeps from reinventing wheel

3. Identify anything that could significantly affect (or be affected by) the project.

- o What other projects, if any, overlap with your team's project? Could their activities or deliverables affect your project?

- o What projects will be affected by your project but are not the responsibility of your team?

- o What projects will supply inputs to your project?

- o Are there any initiatives, legal matters, or pending regulatory matters that could affect your project?

- o Also ask the sponsor, stakeholder groups, project customer, or team for ideas.

3-Day Conference

The department that is affected by the 3-day conference, but is not directly a part of the project scope is:

- Human Resource Department is affected because new hires who will work on projects can be informed of the conference so they can register, since the planned announcements may precede their arrival.

Be very clear on the breadth and depth of your project team's responsibilities. Unless the team has approval from the project sponsor, it should not get involved in other processes or projects that need improvement.

Watch out for other projects that are working on a deliverable that could affect your project team's activities. For example, suppose another team is creating a procedure for using purchasing cards, and your team is redesigning the purchasing system. The other team's deliverable (the purchasing card) could have a major impact on your project. In this case, invite someone from the other team to advise your project, or ask your project sponsor to provide direction on how to integrate the two projects.

4. Record the information in a project boundaries analysis.

Project Boundaries Analysis Report		
Step 1	Items/areas included *(List)*	Why?
	Items not included	Why?
Step 2	Stakeholders/departments to include: *(List)*	Why?
Step 3	Projects, initiatives, events *(List)*	Why?

 Ask your sponsor, other project managers, and new team members to review this analysis and update it periodically.

Create a Work Breakdown Structure (WBS) of Subprojects and Accountability

Why do it?

To divide the work of the project and assign activities to subprojects. The WBS shows at a glance which subprojects will be conducted and who will be held accountable for making sure the work is done. To create the WBS, you use the following items developed during scope planning:

- ○ Final and organizational deliverables
- ○ Interim deliverables

Subproject teams and members then convert the work assignments into their own subproject plans.

How do I do it?

1. Create the list of subprojects.

   ○ A subproject represents a chunk of work that will be overseen by a project team member or subproject leader.

   ○ Subprojects should be aligned with the way the work of the project will be done or how the organization breaks down work (functional areas). Or you can organize the project by one of the following:
      ○ Geography
      ○ Product line or line of business
      ○ Customer
      ○ Project phase
      ○ Industry
      ○ Calendar

   ○ Subprojects may also include work that is performed by vendors, subcontractors, or others. The subproject is accountable to make sure the work is completed on time and meets the acceptance criteria. If a subproject involves procurement or your supply chain, be sure to coordinate with those groups as appropriate.

 Include a subproject called "Project Management." This subproject includes the reports (project charter, project management plan, status reports, project closeout report, etc.) and deliverables that will be produced by the project as a whole, along with any items that don't fit another subproject, especially the project's final deliverable.

2. Create a WBS of the subprojects.

   ○ To create the WBS, you will use the following items developed during scope planning:
      ○ Final and organizational deliverables
      ○ Interim deliverables

- Write the name of the project on the left edge of a piece of flip chart paper.
- On the first tier of branches, write the names of the subprojects.

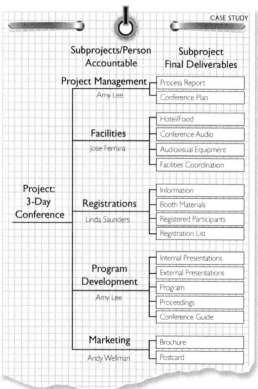

Subprojects/Person Accountable	Subproject Final Deliverables
Project Management Amy Lee	Process Report Conference Plan
Facilities Jose Ferrara	Hotel/Food Conference Audio Audiovisual Equipment Facilities Coordination
Project: 3-Day Conference / **Registrations** Linda Saunders	Information Booth Materials Registered Participants Registration List
Program Development Amy Lee	Internal Presentations External Presentations Program Proceedings Conference Guide
Marketing Andy Wellman	Brochure Postcard

If you're on a webinar, use a whiteboard to sketch the tree/WBS format. If you're on a teleconference, use a Visio or Excel file for the team to record their ideas for discussion.

3. Assign a team member to lead each subproject.

   ○ The person who leads a subproject is accountable for it.

   ○ Add the name of the accountable person on the next subproject branch to the right. Only one person should be accountable for each subproject.

   ○ The project manager is accountable for the "Project Management" subproject and the overall project.

For a large, complex subproject, it may be a good idea to create a charter and project management plan for that subproject.

4. Define the final deliverables that each subproject will produce.

   ○ Each subproject should identify the final deliverables the subproject will produce.

   ○ Write the names of these deliverables on the next branch to the right of each subproject.

5. Review the list of interim deliverables for the project, and make sure that each one is included in the WBS.

If the interim deliverable is produced by the project as a whole, place it in the "Project Management" branch. These interim deliverables are usually produced as a result of several subproject activities.

3-Day Conference

The conference plan is an interim project deliverable that does not belong in any of the subprojects. It is a synthesis of the plans created by each subproject. The sticky note for "conference plan" belongs with the sub-project called "Project Management."

6. Review the WBS.

- ○ Are there any duplicate deliverables? If the same deliverable appears in more than one subproject, decide which duplicate to keep. Then eliminate the others from the WBS.

- ○ Have any deliverables been overlooked? If so, add them to the appropriate subproject.

- ○ Do a "sanity check" to verify the WBS looks right.

Analyze the Project Risks

All projects have some risk. A *risk* is an uncertain event that positively or negatively impacts project objectives. *Project objectives* are the goals for the project; positive effects are opportunities, and negative effects are threats to the project objectives.

Project risk analysis is the process of comparing the risk level to the risk limit given in the project charter. The risk level is determined by analyzing the risk events, project objectives, and risk responses.

Project risk overall is the risk of not meeting project objectives. It falls into three typical categories.

- *Scope risk* is the risk of not meeting the acceptance criteria for the final deliverable (scope objective).
- *Schedule risk* is the risk of not meeting the project deadline (schedule objective).
- *Cost risk* is the risk of not meeting the approved project budget (cost objective).

 There can be additional project objectives, depending on your project. Make sure you know how "success" will be measured.

In a Nutshell:
Project Objectives and Project Risks

Project Objective	Type of Risk Analysis	Defined in the Project Management Plan as...	Measured by:
Scope	Scope risk analysis	• Deliverables • Scope description	Acceptance criteria
Schedule	Schedule risk analysis	• Milestone schedule • Deliverables schedule	Deadline dates
Cost	Cost risk analysis	• Cost estimates • Effort estimates	Approved budgets

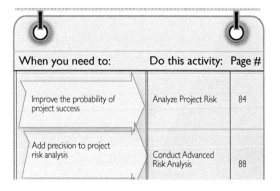

When you need to:	Do this activity:	Page #
Improve the probability of project success	Analyze Project Risk	84
Add precision to project risk analysis	Conduct Advanced Risk Analysis	88

Analyze Project Risk

Why do it?

To improve the probability of project success and to determine whether the degree of risk is acceptable. By sharing the risk analysis with people outside the project, the team demonstrates its competence to the project sponsor, customer, and stakeholders.

How do I do it?

1. Prepare for project risk analysis.

   ○ Write the name of the project's final deliverable on a sticky note. Place it, and the acceptance criteria, at the top of a flip chart.

   ○ Discuss the risk limit with the project sponsor. (This limit should be in the project charter; verify that it has not changed.)

Don't forget to analyze the risk for organizational and operational deliverables, and add your risk responses to the project management plan.

Draw on a whiteboard, or create a file or online document to resemble the flip chart format.

2. Identify the risk events.
    ○ Make sure the team understands the objectives.
    ○ Brainstorm the risk events, writing each risk on a sticky note.

Brainstorm as many events as possible. For tips on brainstorming, see Chapter 3.

3. Process the risk events.
    ○ Discuss and understand the risk events.
    ○ Assign a risk level to each risk event. Use a scale from 1–10, with 10 = highest risk, 1 = lowest.

Risk Level

The *risk level* is the project's risk in a quantified form. When you determine the risk level, take into account how vulnerable your objectives are, considering the opportunities and threats you face.

If there is a way to reduce the risk level to a level lower than the risk limit—without adding costs such as time, money, or much effort—include it. Otherwise, put the additional risk responses on the issues list and then discuss them with the project sponsor.

---

4. Determine your risk responses.

   ○ Brainstorm possible risk responses using Write it, Say it, Slap it (see Chapter 3).

 Risk responses are the options and actions that enhance (or exploit) opportunities and reduce threats to the project.

   ○ Discuss the responses. Determine the ones to add the project management plan.

Types of Risk Responses

Risk Response	Description
Accept	Do not change the project management plan, because there is no suitable response.
Avoid	Change the project management plan to eliminate the risk or the impact.
Mitigate	Change the project management plan to reduce probability or impact.
Transfer	Contractually or physically transfer the impact of the risk and ownership of the response to another party (e.g., buy insurance) or location.

5. Determine new risk levels, and assign accountability for each risk response.

   ○ Given the risk responses you have chosen, reanalyze the risk level.

   ○ Assign someone to be accountable for responding to each risk.

   ○ Add this information to a risk analysis report (also known as a risk register).

Risk Analysis for the 3-Day Conference

Deliverable: Project Management Conference
Acceptance Criteria: Evaluations = rating of at least 4 out of 5 attendees
Project Risk Limit: Low

Risk Events	Risk Level	Risk Responses Countermeasures	Revised Risk Level	Person Accountable for Risk Response
Not enough speakers agree to present at the conference	Medium	Offer an Honorarian	Low	Amy Lee
Speakers are not of high enough quality	Medium	Offer to publish papers in a monthly magazine	Low	Amy Lee
Speakers do not show up (travel problems)	Medium	Have back-up speakers	Low	Amy Lee
Qualified speakers do not know about our conference	High	Find industry trade associations and partners who can send the email to potential speakers	Medium	Andy Wellman

Benefits of Project Risk Analysis

- Performing a risk analysis increases the credibility of the project management plan and the sponsor's confidence in the project team's ability to success-fully complete the project.

- The objectives must be defined to properly complete a risk analysis. If not crystal-clear, work with the sponsor to clarify.

- Involving people outside the project team (senior management, stakeholder groups, customers and suppliers to the project, etc.) helps build political support for the project, and improves the quality of the risk analysis.

Be on the lookout for changes, inside and outside your organiza-tion, that could affect your project risk. Look for changes in the scope of the project or changes in the environment (organizational, regulatory, competitive, or technological). Whenever these changes occur—during planning or execution—perform another risk analysis.

Conduct Advanced Risk Analysis

Why do it?

To add precision to project risk analysis by including both the probability and the impact of project risks.

Quality/customer satisfaction, cost/money, schedule/time—this is the language of management. It is what they understand. When you're negotiating for project success, supply management with data about these project elements.

How do I do it?

1. Follow steps 1 and 2 of the risk analysis process discussed earlier.

2. Create a grid (as shown next) that reflects the impact and probability of risks.

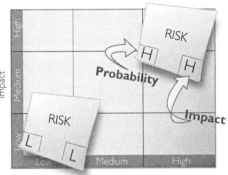

Probability

3. Analyze each risk, and place the sticky note for each risk on the grid according to probability and impact.

4. Analyze and assign a risk level to each risk.

   ○ Assign a number from 1 to 10, with 10 representing the highest impact or greatest probability. Put probability in lower left corner, impact in lower right corner.

   ○ As before, 1–3 = low; 4–7 = moderate; 8–10 = high

5. Determine new risk levels, and assign accountability for each risk response (repeat step 5 on page 86).

For more on advanced risk analysis, see *The Advanced Project Management Memory Jogger™*

Prepare a Project Quality Plan

There are two aspects to *quality*: doing the right things (fitness for use) and doing them right (conformance to specifications). You can improve project outcomes by integrating quality activities and principles into the project process and the project management plan.

Some quality management techniques are best suited for repetitive transactions (such as processing or manufacturing) that provide data to support continuous improvement of processes and products. In contrast, projects are usually one off; the deliverable is created only once, and the project is completed. As a result, project teams have little opportunity to improve the quality of the deliverable or the project process during the project.

Many deliverables—interim or final—are improved by undergoing a technical review or approval process or by additional monitoring to make sure things are proceeding as planned. For many projects, the risk analysis, along with a table of reviews and approvals (described in this section), will suffice for a project quality plan.

Depending on the nature of the project, you may need additional items such as a critical items list and materials and equipment lists—whatever is needed to ensure a successful project.

When you need to:	Do this activity:	Page #
Ensure the quality of project deliverables and project process	Develop a Project Quality Plan	91

Develop a Project Quality Plan

Why do it?

To help coordinate quality activities to successfully meet the project objectives.

How do I do it?

1. Complete and publish the risk analysis report, as explained in the preceding section.

2. Create a reviews and approvals table that includes the following:
   ○ The name of each deliverable
   ○ The name of the person accountable to produce the deliverable
   ○ The purpose of the review or approval
   ○ The names of the participants who will provide input to the review or approval
   ○ The relevant dates

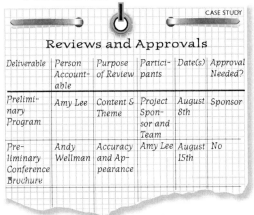

CASE STUDY

Reviews and Approvals

Deliverable	Person Account-able	Purpose of Review	Partici-pants	Date(s)	Approval Needed?
Preliminary Program	Amy Lee	Content & Theme	Project Sponsor and Team	August 8th	Sponsor
Preliminary Conference Brochure	Andy Wellman	Accuracy and Appearance	Amy Lee	August 15th	No

3. Include any required reviews or approvals from the charter or sponsor.

   ❍ Minimize the number of reviews. Make sure each one will add real value to the project.

4. Review the table with your team. Ask, "Will this be adequate to ensure quality?"

   ❍ Ensure that the team understands the risks and determines whether a review or approval would help.

5. Include these dates in the project schedule (discussed in this chapter, page 101).

   ❍ If you need people outside the team to participate in reviews, notify them so they can plan to participate.

 When you update the project sponsor and customer on the project's status through reviews and/or approvals, it can be politically useful for building and maintaining their support for the project.

Prepare a Project Procurement Plan

Procurement is often taken for granted, because most people believe they already know how to buy things. But some projects require significant and sophisticated procurement skills. The project may need to purchase numerous, long-lead-time, expensive items that are critical to the success of the project.

The *project procurement plan* typically includes a critical items list and a list of materials and equipment (spreadsheet or database). Once you have identified the required procurement activities and deliverables, these items will be a component of the project management plan. If procurement is a significant part of the project, make it a subproject; the final deliverables of the procurement subproject are the delivered items.

When you need to:	Do this activity:	Page #
Ensure that the project has the needed materials, equipment, and other items	Develop a Project Procurement Plan	93

Develop a Project Procurement Plan

Why do it?

To ensure that the project team obtains the items needed to meet project objectives.

How do I do it?

1. Scope the procurement for the project.

   ○ Determine what you will need to obtain to complete the project, including equipment, facilities, services, and contractors.

   ○ Determine the best sources of these items.

      ○ Equipment: make or buy, rent, new or used? Off-the-shelf or customized?

      ○ Services: hire contractors, use internal resources, or outsource the work?

A spreadsheet or database is the best way to keep track of the items that need to be procured. The document may be called a materials and equipment list, a purchase order register, or a contracts list. Procurement, or the purchasing or supply chain department representative, should be a member of the project team, if successful procurement is critical to the project (the items are costly, highly risky, or critical to schedule).

- ❍ Managing a large purchase order or contract with a supplier can be treated as a subproject of the project or part of the procurement sub-project.
- ❍ The subproject should deliver all the key elements of a project plan (schedule, reviews and approvals, etc.) to the subproject leader so that she can manage the vendor.

2. Prepare the requisition documents for procurement.

- ❍ Include technical descriptions: specifications, features and functions, quantities, acceptance criteria, and quality control requirements.
- ❍ State the commercial terms: payment terms, cancellation fee schedule, and legal, insurance, and liability issues.

Your project can be canceled without warning, for any number of reasons. Find out your financial liability at certain points in the supplier's schedule if this should happen. If you don't have this information when the order is placed, you are at the mercy of the vendor if you cancel the order. You always have more influence and leverage *before* the order is placed.

- ❍ Describe the supplier's status-reporting requirements, schedule, plan for delivery (primarily for custom equipment), and requirements for documentation, inspections, and reviews.

3. Issue a request for proposal (RFP).

- ❍ Use prequalified suppliers, or qualify the supplier.

Consider a site visit to inspect the facilities and assess the supplier's management team as needed.

- ○ Technical capability: quality control procedures, experience
- ○ Business performance: financial stability, business continuity, reputation, track record, references
- ○ Schedule performance: meeting promised delivery dates, capability to meet promised dates

4. Evaluate the proposals.
- ○ Use a spreadsheet to evaluate proposals.

Use Prioritization Matrices, as explained in Appendix B to choose the best supplier when comparing proposals.

- ○ Develop and prioritize criteria for selecting the best suppliers.
- ○ Negotiate as needed, and select the supplier.

5. Award the purchase order or contract, and manage, expedite, and ensure supplier quality.
- ○ Determine progress reporting requirements.
- ○ Conduct acceptance tests and reviews and approvals.

Allow for procurement lead time in the project schedule. It is often a good idea to inquire about delivery times early in planning, before you are ready to specify and purchase the item.

Review Project Team Membership

Having the right people on your project team can mean the difference between project success and setback. The project charter may specify the initial team, but you need to analyze team membership periodically during planning and execution to meet changing needs. In this activity, you review the composition of the project team to verify that you have the needed skills and expertise and that the project's stakeholders and interests are represented.

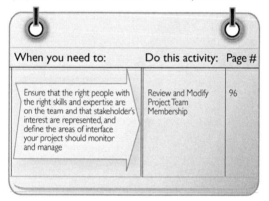

When you need to:	Do this activity:	Page #
Ensure that the right people with the right skills and expertise are on the team and that stakeholder's interest are represented, and define the areas of interface your project should monitor and manage	Review and Modify Project Team Membership	96

Review and Modify Team Membership

Why do it?

To identify the skills, expertise, and relationships required to complete the project. To ensure that the right people are involved at the appropriate level.

How do I do it?

1. Identify the skills and expertise required to create the deliverables and manage the risks.

To verify that you have a clear understanding of the project's deliverables and risks, review the risk analysis and WBS.

2. Identify the stakeholders who should be represented on the project team.

  ○ Stakeholders include people in the departments or functional areas that are affected by the project. They may also include customers and suppliers.

  ○ Determine the best *membership status* for each stakeholder and team member: regular, ad hoc, or liaison (see "Team Membership Status" below).

Not all of the project's stakeholders have to be on the team. Consider each stakeholder group, and decide how to best manage each group. This can be done through communication and project status reports; they don't have to attend the meetings.

Team Membership Status

People can participate on the project team in three ways: as *regular* team members (who attend all team meetings); as *ad hoc* members (who participate only when needed); or as *liaisons* (who serve as contacts with a stakeholder, stakeholder group, or another project).

Assign regular team membership status to those who need to participate in all team meetings. Remember that you can bring people into the process at any time on an ad hoc basis, or you can keep them up to date through a liaison. And as the nature of the work changes over time, regular members may change to ad hoc or liaison status.

Team Status	Description
Regular (full participation)	Attends all project team meetings while on the project
Ad hoc (part time)	Attends project team meetings as needed — e.g., a subject matter expert
Liaison (a team member who covers a stakeholder group or another project)	Provides structured, proactive, targeted communication to a stakeholder or or another project

Teams are most productive when they include four to seven people. Try to limit your meetings to a maximum of ten people. Take advantage of the liaison role; assign a team member to manage stakeholders according to how much they are affected and how much influence they have. A greatly affected and highly influential group or person requires more attention.

CASE STUDY

In our case study, Ralph Panetta originally was a regular team member, but during planning the project team decided to include his department in the "Marketing" and "Program Development" subprojects. Now Ralph doesn't need to be a regular member of the project team. Instead, he will serve as an ad hoc member of the two subproject teams.

Key Stakeholders of the 3-Day Conference

Skills Required, Stakeholder, or Area	Team Member Name	Team Member Status (Regular, Ad Hoc, Liaison)	Team Member Liaison Name (if applicable)
Facilities	Jose Ferrara	Regular	N/A
Marketing	Andy Wellman	Regular	N/A
Member Services	Linda Saunders	Regular	N/A
New Product Development	Amy Lee	Regular	N/A
~~Graphic Design and Printing~~	~~Ralph Panotta~~	~~Regular~~	~~N/A~~
The Madison Hotel	None	None	Jose Ferrara
Audiovisual Company	None	None	Jose Ferrara
Rhonda Levinson (Legal Counsel)	None	None	Amy Lee

To determine the areas and stakeholders to consider, refer to "Analyze the Project Boundaries," page 74.

3. Determine whether other departments, functional areas, and projects should be represented on your project team.

   ○ Consider the functional areas and projects that will significantly affect, or be affected by, your project. Those who will participate in project team meetings should be regular team members.

   ○ To identify the affected areas and projects, see "Analyze the Project Boundaries."

   ○ If the area or project doesn't require a team member (regular or ad hoc), assign someone to act as a liaison.

CASE STUDY

Departments and Projects Affected by the 3-Day Conference

Department or Project	Team Representative	Team Status	Team Member Liaison
Project management process project	None	None	Amy Lee
Billing process improvement project	Lyle Yendow	Ad Hoc	None
Human resource department	None	None	Amy Lee

4. Assess the current team for the skills and relationships you need to meet the project's objectives.
   - ○ If you lack any needed expertise, add that to the issues list for the project manager to resolve with the sponsor.
   - ○ Negotiate with functional managers or the project sponsor to obtain the right people.

5. Periodically review and modify your project team membership.
   - ○ If the project scope changes, revisit team membership to verify that you have the right people participating at the right level.

 If you don't have the right skills on your project team, you can use this analysis when you negotiate for new team members, training, outside consultants, or other means to close the skills gap. Be sure to quantify and emphasize the impact on the project's deliverables and risk level in your negotiations.

Create a Project Schedule

The value of creating a project schedule is to demonstrate how the project will meet the project deadlines. A *milestone schedule* shows the dates the major steps will be completed. A *deliverables schedule* shows the delivery dates for all the project deliverables, along with the interdependencies.

 Interdependent means that two or more things are dependent on each other. Example: B cannot start until A is finished or completed. This interdependency is called a "finish—start."

Once a schedule is completed, the information can be entered into a project management software program, which will give the team a way to update and monitor the schedule as the project progresses.

When you need to:	Do this activity:	Page #
Set interim goals that will help the team measure its progress toward the final deliverables	Construct a Milestone Schedule	102
Show the delivery dates for each deliverable and specify who is accountable for each one	Create a Deliverables Schedule	106

Construct a Milestone Schedule

Why do it?

To establish dates and deadlines that will guide the project team's progress toward its ultimate goal. The milestone schedule is the foundation of all the other project schedules. It shows the sequence of major accomplishments and the dates they need to be completed.

How do I do it?

1. Define the start date for the project and the date that the team expects to close out the project.

   o A project usually starts when the project manager receives the project charter. If the project sponsor doesn't provide a charter, then the start date is the day when the team begins to create a charter of its own.

- ○ Record the date that you expect the project to be closed out.
- ○ A project is closed out after the sponsor has accepted the closeout report.

2. Record the dates when you expect the project charter and project management plan to be approved.

3. Add the deadline dates for each final deliverable.

- ○ The deadline dates for the final deliverables should be provided in the project charter. If these dates were not provided, decide when each deliverable can and should be completed.

- ○ Deadline dates may not be the same as completion dates. The _deadline date_ is the date when the customer expects to receive the final deliverable. The _completion date_ is the date when the team estimates the final deliverable will be complete.

4. Add milestones for the execution of the project, and assign a completion date for each milestone.

- ○ Review the list of interim deliverables, select the most significant ones, and estimate their completion dates. (For more on determining the interim deliverables, see page 72.)

 Limit the total number of execution milestones to 10. If there are more than 10 execution milestones, use only those that represent the most significant accomplishments for the project.

 Deadlines are usually assigned by the project sponsor or customer, and milestones are assigned by the project team. Milestones are targets and are flexible, but deadlines must be met.

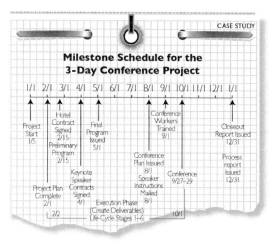

CASE STUDY

Milestone Schedule for the
3-Day Conference Project

| 1/1 | 2/1 | 3/1 | 4/1 | 5/1 | 6/1 | 7/1 | 8/1 | 9/1 | 10/1 | 11/1 | 12/1 | 1/1 |

Project Start 1/5

Hotel Contract Signed 2/15
Preliminary Program 2/15

Final Program Issued 5/1

Conference Workers Trained 9/1

Closeout Report Issued 12/31

Conference Plan Issued 8/1

Process report Issued 12/31

Project Plan Complete 2/1

Keynote Speaker Contracts Signed 4/1

Conference Speaker Instructions Mailed 8/1

Conference 9/27-29

2/2

Execution Phase (Create Deliverables) Life-Cycle Stages 1-6

10/1

5. Perform an initial schedule risk analysis.

   ○ This process is similar to the project risk analysis you performed earlier.

   ○ Identify risks that can prevent you from meeting the deadlines.

   ○ Analyze the risks you have identified.

   ○ Develop risk responses to mitigate the impact and/or probability of the risks.

   ○ Assign accountability to team members for implementing the risk responses.

   ○ After the risk responses are chosen, if the team's risk level is 4 or higher, reexamine the assumptions that the team made in creating the milestone schedule. List any risk responses that could be used to decrease the risk of not meeting the deadline dates.

○ If the team cannot lower its risk level to at least 3, add this item to the issues list so that the project manager and the project sponsor can discuss it.

Schedule Risk Level
3-Day Conference

The deadline dates for the final deliverable, i.e., the conference, are September 27, 28, and 29. Team members agreed on a risk level of 1 because they are confident that all of the necessary activities will be completed before these dates because the suppliers have agreed to their committed dates.

Don't forget to set a risk level for each organizational deliverable. For example, in our sample project the deadline date for the "Project Management Process Report" is December 31. The team decided there would be sufficient time to prepare the report after the conference was held, so this deliverable was given a risk level of 2.

The milestone schedule may be the only schedule needed for your project, and the only one the project sponsor, customer, and stakeholders see, so include the dates and items that they are concerned about.

Create a Deliverables Schedule

A *deliverables schedule* shows the sequence of deliverables to be created, from first to last, and identifies who is accountable for meeting the delivery date for each deliverable.

Why do it?

To help the team determine the flow of project work, identify predecessors and accountability, and see the big picture. A deliverables schedule provides a baseline for executing the project and monitoring the schedule during execution and serves as a road map for completing the deliverables, including the completion dates.

 For this activity, refer to the work breakdown structure (WBS) you created earlier.

 If a subproject team is creating its own deliverables schedule, add that team's milestone dates to the project's milestone dates listed along the timeline.

How do I do it?

1. Create a deliverables schedule diagram.
    - Tape three or four pieces of flip chart paper in portrait (vertical) orientation.
    - Put the milestone schedule on the bottom (X-axis).
    - List the subprojects on the left side (Y-axis).
    - Put the subproject final deliverables on the right side of the diagram.

Creating a Deliverables Schedule
Step 1

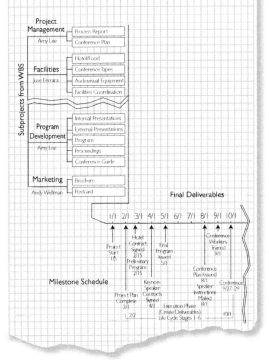

2. Write the name of each deliverable (interim and final) on a 3×3 sticky note.

  ○ Create a sticky note for each interim and final deliverable on the WBS.

  ○ Put the following information on each note:

    ○ Subproject name or abbreviation. For example, you might indicate "Marketing" with the letter M.

    ○ Identification number (optional)

    ○ Deliverable name

    ○ Person accountable

    ○ Leave space in the lower-right corner of the note to add a delivery date. If a deliverable already has a deadline or date constraint, add it to the sticky note now.

    ○ Duration (calendar time from start to completion—e.g., two weeks)

    ○ Predecessor (deliverable or event) put on top right corner.

It will save time if team members create the sticky notes for their subprojects and then bring them to the team meeting.

Don't forget to complete sticky notes for organizational deliverables, including interim organizational deliverables.

3. Place the sticky notes on the right side of the diagram, in chronological order by subproject.

  ○ Align the final deliverables with their delivery dates (along the timeline) and with the correct branches of the subproject tree (along the side of the diagram).

What Goes on the Sticky Notes?

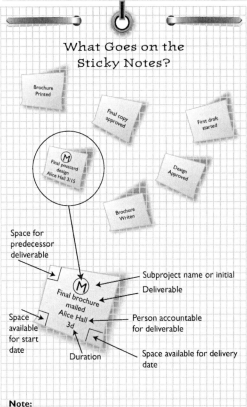

Note:
No delivery dates for the deliverables of the "Marketing" subproject have been assigned yet.

- ○ Align the interim deliverables with the final deliverables and the timeline.
- ○ Give each subproject its own swim lane or row.

4. Move the notes left to the appropriate points on the diagram based on the milestones.

- ○ First, try to align the interim deliverables with the milestone dates. If that doesn't work, align the interim deliverables so that the final deliverable dates are met, and then revise the milestone dates (unless the date is a deadline).

5. Connect the deliverables with arrows.

- ○ Draw arrows from each interim deliverable to the next interim or final deliverable in the chain. Arrows represent predecessor relationships.

 Arrows should enter the left side and exit the right side when possible. All lines should go from left to right, never right to left.

 If a predecessor to a deliverable comes from an outside party or vendor, then the affected subproject team (and its leader), as well as procurement, is accountable for making sure it is received on time.

6. Determine the start and completion dates for each deliverable.

- ○ Use a calendar, and count only the working days available to complete the deliverables.
- ○ Holidays and weekends are usually nonworking days.
- ○ Be sure to consider vacations and other events that can affect delivery dates.
- ○ Consult with the team to determine whether they can meet these dates.
- ○ Here are two ways to determine start and completion dates:

Partial Deliverables Schedule for the 3-Day Conference Project

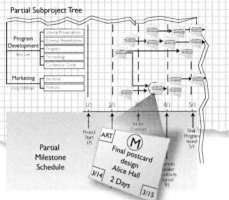

Partial Subproject Tree

Program Development — Amy Lee
- Internal Presentations
- External Presentations
- Program
- Preroaching
- Conference Guide

Marketing — Andy Welling
- Brochure
- Postcard

Partial Milestone Schedule

Project Start 1/5

ART — Final postcard design — Alice Hall — 2 Days — 3/14 — 3/15

Hotel Contract

Final Program Issued 5/1

- A deliverable's completion is dependent on the completion date of the predecessor and the duration required to create the deliverable. (This is also called As Soon As Possible— the default method for most scheduling software.)
- The date when the person accountable can commit to completing the deliverable.

7. Review the major milestones, and revise as necessary.

- If the milestones are not deadlines, change the milestones to match the completion dates you have just calculated.
- If a deadline cannot be met, use schedule compression techniques to meet the deadline.
- If the deadline cannot be met, discuss it with the project sponsor or customer.

Schedule Compression Techniques:
Ways to Finish Earlier

Schedule Problem:	Try This:
End date past deadline	• Create concurrent deliverables • Increase resources
Interim deliverable too late for next (successor) deliverable	• Break interim deliverable into smaller deliverables (decompose) • Shift date of next deliverable if the deadline cannot be met. Verify this is OK with the owner of the successor • Decrease scope
Disagreement over durations	• Verify assumptions used to estimate dates • Increase detail • Ask a third party or an expert to review
Can't meet deadlines	• Negotiate deadlines with the project customer and/or project sponsor • Negotiate scope requirements with project customer and/or sponsor • Rework the critical path

The Critical Path

The *critical path* is the minimum time to complete a project, given the sequence and duration for producing the deliverables per the schedule.

Any deliverable *on the critical path will delay the project* completion date if that deliverable is completed later than planned (unless something is changed). In other words, to stay on schedule, you must make sure that any items on the critical path are completed on schedule.

For more, see *The Advanced Project Management Memory Jogger*™

One way to tell whether a date is a major milestone is to look for places in the schedule where several deliverables feed into another deliverable. This indicates that several parts of the project have come together. Milestones, however, must ultimately be chosen based on the team's, sponsor's, and customers perceptions of the most important accomplishments of the project.

When people are assigned to multiple projects and also have regular job duties, often they must resolve conflicting priorities. As a result, the completion dates that they can commit to may not be compatible with the project's deadlines. In this case, talk to the project sponsor. For more, see *The Advanced Project Memory Jogger*™.

8. Perform a schedule risk analysis.

- ○ Now that the team has more detailed information about the completion dates and interdependencies, these dates should be more accurate.

- ○ To complete this analysis, see page 86, step 5.

- ○ If the team cannot lower its risk level to at least 3, add it to the issues list for the project manager and sponsor to discuss.

 In choosing the best risk responses, the team should base its decisions on the project trade-off decision criteria: lower cost, earlier delivery, or more features. For example, if the schedule takes precedence over the budget, then any risk responses that ensure the schedule is met are good options, even if they cost more.

 Place an asterisk on the sticky notes where the customers' acceptance criteria for the deliverable need to be clarified. Get agreement on the criteria outside the team meeting. The criteria should be written down as part of the documentation for the project management plan.

Calculate the Project's Contingency

Contingency reserve (or simply *contingency*) is an amount of time, money, or effort you should add to the estimates you make on your project, as discussed in the following sections. Even the best estimates are just that—estimates. Determining the amount of contingency you need to add is a combination of art and science.

 They call it an "estimate" for a reason. All estimates are only guesses, although some are better than others. Even if very accurate, an estimate is still an approximation based on assumptions and limited information that is often collected early in the project.

Fat, slush, cushion, and padding are some of the uncomplimentary terms for contingency. Some of them imply that this added amount is a bad thing. Unfortunately, many project managers believe that they need to hide the contingency in their estimates; otherwise, they believe, the project sponsor or customer will remove it.

That's not a good idea. Instead, you should educate your management about the need for contingency and the accuracy of your estimates so that they will understand why you need to add contingency to be successful. Otherwise, when the unexpected happens, your project may miss its estimates.

It is a good practice to have a contingency management process. Some project managers use an internal change management or change control system similar to the one they use to formally change the project management plan.

Why do it?

To allocate time, money, or effort to respond to errors in estimating your project's resource needs.

How do I do it?

1. Review your project risk analysis.

   ○ Assess the level of risk that could impact your ability to meet the project objectives for schedule, effort, and cost.

2. Ask the team members how much contingency, if any, is already included in their estimates of duration, effort hours, and costs.

Project team members generally include some contingency in their estimates, so it's a good idea to ask them whether they have done so. Be careful not to duplicate contingency in individual items and in the contingency reserve.

3. Review your estimates, your assumptions, and specific risk events that could impact the project outcomes.

4. If the accuracy of your estimate is low to medium, or if the risk level is medium to high, then consider adding contingency to the estimate, "just because" no estimate is exact.

5. Consult with peers, your sponsor, and the project team and use expert judgment to determine how much contingency to add.

 A simple way to estimate contingency is by percentage of the total duration. For a low-risk project, 10% may be adequate; for a high-risk project, you may need 25%. Extremely long or short projects may require a different percentage of contingency for the same risk level, and you may need to adjust the amount. For example, a two-month project may need two weeks' contingency (25%). A six-month project of the same risk level may need only three weeks of contingency, or less than 15%. Instead of a percentage, you can use a fixed amount (e.g., a week or a month) or a combination of the two.

To increase commitment, buy in, and accuracy, be sure to include your project team members in the estimating process and get their input.

6. Develop a process and policy for allocating contingency reserve.

   ○ If you have a project change management process (discussed later in this chapter), use it to document and allocate contingency. If you don't have such a process, you will need to develop one. During execution, monitor your project risks and performance, and adjust the amount of contingency as needed.

Where Should Contingency Reside?

Many people prefer to build contingency into each deliverable on the schedule. Although this is a common practice, it increases the length of the project because this contingency will almost certainly be used, whether or not the reason for it has occurred. Instead, you should place your project contingency in a common reserve. In that way, the total amount of contingency is generally less than if it were included in every deliverable. To effectively manage the contingency reserve, use a project change management process to allocate the contingency when it is needed.

The Advanced Project Management Memory Jogger™

Comparison Between Common Reserve and Deliverable Contingency

	Contingency in Common Reserve	Contingency in Each Item
Project duration	Shorter	Longer
Project learning	More documentation and data to support lessons learned.	No documentation regarding contingency. Amount of contingency is not defined nor understood.
Use of contingency	Some contingency may be unused.	All contingency is generally used, and often more is needed.
Management control	Project manager develops and controls contingency, with team input.	Individual team members determine and control contingency.
Planning effectiveness	Schedule dates are recalculated, contingency is adjusted, and risks are monitored during execution.	Completion dates are adjusted when they are missed.

The Advanced Project Management Memory Jogger™

 It is a good practice to have a contingency management process. Some project managers use an internal change management or change control system similar to the one they use to formally change the project management plan.

Estimate the Effort Required for the Project

The *effort* that people in an organization expend on a project can be a major expense. You should estimate the required effort to determine whether you can complete the project within the effort limit.

 Effort is the number of hours worked; *duration* is the calendar or elapsed time.

When you need to:	Do this activity:	Page #
Estimate the total amount of effort to complete a project	Estimate the Total Project Effort	120
Understand the accuracy of the effort estimate	Rate the Accuracy of the Estimate	121
Determine whether the effort estimate is over the limit	Compare the Effort Estimate to the Effort Limit	122
Determine how much and when the effort will be needed and control effort on your project during execution	Create an Effort Forecast	125
Estimate the costs of the project so that the organization knows how much money should be allocated	Create a Project Budget	127

Estimate the Total Project Effort

Why do it?

To estimate the total amount of effort that will be required to complete the project.

How do I do it?

1. Estimate the amount of effort needed for each subproject or each individual who will work on the project.

   - For each individual, multiply the number of hours per week by the number of weeks he will work on the project. To obtain a total amount of effort for the project, add the effort of all workers.

   - For a subproject, the subproject leader, with the help of her team, prepares an estimate of effort for the subproject. To get a total for the project as a whole, combine the total amount of effort from each subproject.

2. Check with your sponsor to see whether any internal resources are considered overhead (not billable to your project).

   - Don't include any overhead effort in your estimate.

   - Don't estimate the effort for any work that is outside the scope of the project.

 You can convert the effort estimate to full-time equivalents (FTEs) as appropriate. Many organizations define one FTE as a fixed number of hours per week or month (usually about 40 hours per week). This is a quick way to communicate the total effort in standard units. Find out how your organization defines an FTE, or how total effort should be presented, effort hours, FTEs, etc.

The effort for each team member should include effort for project activities (attending meetings, preparing reports, or project planning) as well as the effort to create deliverables. Be sure to ask the team to include both kinds of effort in its estimates. It's easy to forget about the time people spend on, for example, meetings and reports.

Rate the Accuracy of the Estimate

Why do it?

To understand how accurate your effort estimates are.

How do I do it?

1. Rate the accuracy of the total effort estimate.

   ○ The accuracy rating indicates how confident the team members are that the estimate is an accurate prediction of how much effort the project will require.

   ○ Use the letters **H**, **M**, and **L** (high, medium, and low) to indicate your team's confidence in the estimate.

   H = actual effort could vary by ±10 % from the estimate

   M = actual effort could vary by ±25% from the estimate

   L = actual effort could vary by ±50% or more from the estimate

   ○ A low accuracy rating means that the team doesn't really know; the estimate is only a guess

   ○ List the reasons for the rating.

Use the percentage ranges that are appropriate for your organization.

If the accuracy rating is medium or low and if the estimate is lower than the effort limit, the team might consider adding more effort to the estimate to cover the uncertainty of the estimate. See "Calculate the Project's Contingency," page 114.

Compare the Effort Estimate to the Effort Limit

If the project team's effort estimate is lower than the project sponsor's effort limit, then the project team believes that the project can be completed within the effort limit. However, if the effort estimate is higher than the effort limit, then the team may need to review the basis for the effort estimate and discuss it with the sponsor.

Why do it?

To determine whether the effort estimate exceeds the project sponsor's effort limit.

How do I do it?

1. Get ready to compare the effort estimate to the effort limit, if any.

   ○ If the project sponsor has not set a limit on effort, the team should review its assumptions in creating the estimate to make sure they are sound and to gain confidence that this is the best estimate the team can make at this time.

2. To compare the estimate to the limit, calculate the range (±) of the estimate based on its accuracy rating.

   ○ For example, if the team has an estimated effort of 100 hours, with a ±10% (high) accuracy rating, the estimate could vary by 10 hours, more or less. The range for the estimate is 90 to 110 hours.

   ○ The range for each accuracy rating—high, medium, or low—is listed on page 121.

3. If the high end of the range is close to the limit—slightly under or slightly over—and if the assumptions for creating the estimate are sound, then the team should move on to the next planning activity.

4. If the high end of the range is either much higher or much lower than the limit, check your assumptions and list the reasons for the deviation from the limit. Put this on the issues list for the project manager to discuss with the project sponsor.

5. Multiply the effort by the designated rate or cost (per hour or FTE) to determine the cost of the effort.

   ○ Example: 30 hours of effort × $50/hour = $1500

Estimates of Effort Required
for the 3-Day Conference

Subproject efforts have been
estimated as follows:

Subproject	Staff Time in Hours
Marketing	250 Hours
Facilities	350 Hours
Registrations	200 Hours
Program Development	475 Hours
Project Management	100 Hours

Total estimate = 1,375 hours = approximately 8 months (M)

1,375 hours/40 (hours per week) = 34.375 weeks
34.375 weeks/4.3 (weeks per month) = 7.99 months

Accuracy rating = Medium (M)

Staff time range for medium rating (± 25%) = 1,030 to 1,720
hours

Reason for rating: There is a general idea of how much
time the project will take because there was a conference
last year. Unfortunately, good records of the actual time that
staff put into the project are not available.

Effort Limit: None

Even though there is no effort limit, the sponsor has asked
our team to monitor the actual hours that are invested in the
project.

Create an Effort Forecast

Why do it?

To define amount of effort required to complete the project, distributed over the life of the project. An *effort forecast* provides data to support the project's request for human resources, and it's useful for tracking whether effort expenditures are ahead of or behind the budgeted amount.

How do I do it?

1. Calculate the amount of effort that each person or subproject will spend on the project by time period (day, week, month, or quarter).

   ○ The time frame used for calculating the forecast depends on the activity level in the project. For example, the project manager of a long-term project with very little ongoing activity may need to monitor effort every month, whereas the project manager of another long-term project with a lot of activity will need to monitor effort every week.

   ○ Subproject leaders should ask each team member to estimate her effort by time period. Then add it together.

 An effort forecast is always a good idea, because it lets the project manager determine earned value. See page 149.

2. If there are staffing conflicts within the project or with other projects or assignments, adjust your effort forecast.

   ○ If you cannot obtain the amount of resources to meet the deadline dates, then put this issue on the issues list so that the project manager and project sponsor can resolve the problem.

3. Add the total and cumulative effort hours for each week, month, or quarter when the effort will be utilized.

   ○ The cumulative total in the final time period should match the total effort estimate.

Effort Forecast for the 3-Day Conference Project

Effort in Hours	Jan.	Feb.	March	April	May	June	July	Aug.	Sept.	Oct.	Nov.	Dec.
Marketing	16	16	42	48	72	32	4	4	4	4	4	4
Facilities	32	10	40	10	4	4	40	60	130	12	4	4
Registrations	4	4	4	4	6	12	18	50	86	4	4	4
Program Development	70	66	75	40	40	40	40	12	80	4	4	10
Project Management	8	8	6	6	6	12	12	8	8	8	8	10
Effort Hours	130	104	167	108	128	100	114	134	308	32	24	26
Cumulative Effort Hours	130	234	401	509	637	737	851	985	1,293	1,325	1,349	1,375

Create a Project Budget

Whenever a project will incur costs, either internally or by external purchase or contracts, the project team should estimate those costs so that the organization knows how much money should be allocated to the project. If it is important for the organization to know when the money will be spent, they should create a spending forecast.

When you need to:	Do this activity:	Page #
Show a breakdown of how money will be spent during the project	Estimate Project Costs	127
Plan cash flow and track spending as it occurs so costs don't exceed the spending limit for the project (earned value)	Create a Spending Forecast	132

Estimate Project Costs

Why do it?

To determine the amount of funds that should be allocated for the internal/external costs of the project. A cost estimate predicts whether the project can be completed within the cost limits set by the project sponsor.

How do I do it?

1. Estimate the cost of effort and the cost of other internal charges, and calculate the total internal cost of the project.

   ○ *Internal costs* are charged to the project's budget. Internal costs may consist of internal supplies, travel, and effort from your team or from parts of the organization that provide deliverables or services for your project.

- ❍ If you don't already know, ask the project sponsor what will be charged to the project.
- ❍ To estimate the total cost of the effort, see step 3.

 Effort may be considered an internal cost, or it may not be included in the project's budget. Check with your sponsor for guidance.

- ❍ To calculate total internal costs, add together the estimate of the effort and the internal charges.

 If you don't know the billing rate for the effort or subproject, ask the project sponsor what rate to use.

2. Estimate any external costs, and calculate the total.

- ❍ *External costs* are purchases made from outside suppliers. Examples include consultants, contract labor, materials and equipment, travel, and rentals.
- ❍ Purchase orders or contracts are normally used to procure items from external sources.

3. To get an estimated total cost for the project, add together the estimated internal/external cost.

 Make sure that all the costs are within the project scope. For example, suppose that as a result of your project, a department in your organization will need to retrain its people or add new equipment, and this is not in your project's scope. If something like this is discovered, add it to the issues list so that it can be resolved with the sponsor.

4. Assign an accuracy rating to each estimate for internal costs, external costs, and the total project cost.

- ❍ The accuracy rating indicates how confident the team is that the estimates accurately predict what will be spent.

○ As you did earlier in estimating effort, use the letters **H**, **M**, and **L** (high, medium, and low) to indicate your team's confidence in the estimate.

H = actual costs could vary by ±10% from the estimates

M = actual costs could vary by ±25% from the estimates

L = actual costs could vary by ±50% or more from the estimates

○ In determining the accuracy of the total estimate for internal costs, consider the accuracy of the estimate of effort required for the project.

○ List the team's reasons for each accuracy rating.

 If an estimate receives an accuracy rating of medium or low and if the estimate is near the cost limit, consider adding more contingency to the budget to cover the uncertainty. See "Calculate the Project's Contingency," page 114.

5. Compare the team's cost estimates to the project sponsor's limits on costs, if any.

○ If the sponsor did not set a cost limit, then you should review your assumptions to make sure they are correct.

○ To compare the estimate to the limit, calculate a range (±) based on the estimate's accuracy rating. For example, if the cost is estimated at $100, with a medium (±25%) accuracy rating, the estimate could vary by $25, more or less. The dollar range for the estimate is $75 to $125. (Examples of ranges for each accuracy rating—high, medium, or low—are listed in step 4.)

○ If the high end of the range is over the limit, list your assumptions and put the issue on the issues list for the project manager to resolve with the project sponsor.

You do not have to use the ranges given in step 4 if your estimate is more accurate. For example, an estimate with a high accuracy rating might be within ±5% instead of ±10%. In this case, you should use ±5%.

Cost Estimates for the 3-Day Conference

Below is the breakdown of the estimated costs, representing the work done in Steps 1–5.

Internal Costs	Cost Items	Staff Time (in Hours)	Hourly Rate	Total Cost
Staffing Costs				
Marketing	N/A	250	$25	$6,250
Facilities	N/A	350	$25	$8,750
Registrations	N/A	200	$25	$5,000
Program Development	N/A	475	$25	$11,875
Project Management	N/A	100	$25	$2,500
			Subtotal	**$34,375**
Other Internal Costs				
Marketing Materials	Brochures postcards	N/A	N/A	$25,000
			Subtotal	**$25,000**
Estimated total internal costs				**$59,375 M**

Reason for medium rating:
More than 50% of the internal costs are staffing costs and the staff time estimate was given a medium accuracy rating.

Continued...

External Costs	Cost Items	Staff Time (in Hours)	Hourly Rate	Total Cost
Hotel (staff)	The Madison	N/A	N/A	$10,000
Food (based on 300 people)	The Madison	N/A	N/A	$42,400
Audiovisual Company	TBD	N/A	N/A	$25,000
Travel	Staff/speaker travel	N/A	N/A	$5,000
Contingency reserve				$3,000
Estimated total external costs (Range = ± 5% or $4,270)				$85,400 H ($81,130 to $89,670)

Reasons for high rating:
The cost for the hotel and food are established by contractual agreements and audiovisual costs are based on prior experience. Travel expenses are variable, depending on the speakers selected and their locations, so a contingency reserve has been added to the budget to allow for the uncertainty.

Estimated total project costs	$144,775

Sponsor's Cost Limit:
$90,000 for external costs only.
The team's estimate for external costs is **$85,400** and was assigned a high accuracy rating equivalent to a ±5% range, so the upper range of the estimate ($89,670) is under the sponsor's limit.

Create a Spending Forecast

Why do it?

To predict when the project costs will be realized. The spending forecast specifies the amounts and dates of expenditures and provides data for monitoring the project spending.

How do I do it?

1. Assign the project costs to the week, month, or quarter in which the cost will be committed or actually spent.

   ○ An easy way to distribute the costs is to match each cost to a deliverable in the deliverables schedule. Then write the costs under the appropriate time period at the bottom of the chart. In this way, the team can see the schedule and costs by time period in one chart.

   ○ Add the total/cumulative costs for each time period.

CASE STUDY

Spending Forecast for the 3-Day Conference

The table below shows just a part of the spending forecast for the conference

Cost Category	January	February	March	April	May
			(Costs in dollars)		
Staffing Costs	3,250	2,600	4,200	2,700	3,200
Internal Changes			5,000		7,000
External Costs		1,000			
Additional Reserves					
Monthly Total	3,250	3,600	9,200	2,700	10,200
Cumulative Total	3,250	6,850	16,050	18,750	28,950

Create a Communication Plan

You may already have guessed that a great deal of project management has to do with communication. During planning, most of your communication involves the project team, sponsor, and project customers. You also need to plan the key communications you will send out or convey during the entire project. This plan details how the project will communicate with people outside your team.

A *project communication plan* is an organized list of key communications from your project team to various audiences (the project sponsor, project customers, and other stakeholders). It outlines the messages (content), vehicles (methods), timing (schedule), and accountability (ownership) of each key communication.

Why do it?

To identify, define, plan, and schedule appropriate and effective communications.

How do I do it?

1. Identify your audience types.

   ○ Brainstorm the different audiences for your key project communications.

      ○ Project sponsor
      ○ Project customers
      ○ Stakeholders
      ○ Others

 Refer to "Analyze the Project Boundaries," page 74, for stakeholders and topics.

---

2. Identify your key messages for each audience type.

- Consider three types of key messages for the people in that audience:
  - What do you need them to know or understand?
  - What do they need to know or hear from you?
  - What do you want them to do in response to your communication?

3. Determine the best way to deliver each message.

- Consider a variety of methods:
  - Meetings (group discussions, staff meetings)
  - Phone or video conferences
  - E-mails
  - Websites or intranets (posted documents, FAQs)
  - Briefing documents
  - Electronic collaboration tools (online meeting rooms, social media, etc.)
  - One-on-one discussions
- There are two types of communication methods: active and passive.
  - *Active* methods (e.g., meetings, teleconferences) allow for two-way communication and involve interaction between you and your audience.
  - *Passive* methods (e.g., a website) allow only for one-way communication and are more like "broadcasting" information.

4. Determine how you will check for understanding of key messages (as needed).

- Pay particular attention to these kinds of messages:
  - Messages with action items (when you need participation, information sharing, resource assignment, or some other action from the audience)
  - Messages with critical information (when audience confusion could impede your progress or increase your project risk)

○ If checking for understanding is important, write a "Y" (for yes) in the column; if it isn't, write "N" (for no).

 People often broadcast a message to their audience and assume that they've "communicated." Later they're surprised when problems occur because the audience members misunderstood or ignored the message. Communication should be viewed as an outcome, not an event.

5. Package the messages into communication deliverables, and add key communication packages to your project schedule.

○ Identify which messages can be delivered at the same time using the same or multiple methods.

○ Determine whether feedback is part of the package or a separate package.

6. In your project communication plan, include the reasons for and benefits of the changes the project will have on the organization.

○ Tell people what is changing. Work with the appropriate parts of the organization to involve them in developing the messages.

  ○ Connect the changes to the business case.

  ○ First explain the problem, and then explain the solution.

  ○ Do not use jargon.

○ Tell people what will actually be different because of the change.

 The changes may be clear to the project team and to management, but to the people who must make it work, it may be abstract.

 For more about dealing with organizational change, see the next section.

4 | Create a Plan 135

Project Communication Plan
3-Day Conference Example

Audience (team sponsor, customer, stakeholder groups, etc.)	What you want them to know (message)	What you want them to hear (message)	What you want them to do (message)	Method of communication (meetings, teleconference, e-mail, website, intranet, FAQs, cloud collaboration, tools, social media, etc.)	Verify understanding? Yes or No	Date and frequency of communication	Person accountable to prepare and issue
People involved in projects	Conference information	Save the date	Register	E-mail blast intranet	No	When Charter	Andy Wellman
People involved in projects	Program content conference details	Benefits of attending	Register	E-mail webinar intranet	Yes	When final program is approved	Amy Lee Linda Saunders

7. Issue the communication plan, and review and update as needed.
   - ○ Does your feedback tell you that any revision or addition is required?
   - ○ Are the messages and methods effective?
   - ○ Have there been any changes to the project that require adjustments to the communication plan?

Deal with Organizational Change

Projects are temporary and unique, produce new or improved deliverables (a product, service, process, or result), and often include implementation and rollout. Effective project managers understand that these issues involve change, so they help stakeholders adjust to the rollout of a new or revised deliverable. _Organizational change management_ is a set of skills, tools, and techniques to help those who are affected by the project understand and deal with the change it brings.

When you need to:	Do this activity:	Page #
Ensure successful implementation	Plan for Organizational Change	138

Plan for Organizational Change

Why do it?
To address the effects of change on the organization, the project team, and the stakeholders, and to improve the odds of project success.

How do I do it?
1. Determine who is responsible to plan and implement the change—usually the process owner or a member of the project team.

Make sure the project sponsor is providing support as well.

2. In your project management plan, include the key ingredients of change management:
   - An environmental assessment
   - A communication plan
   - Organizational risks and responses
   - Deliverables and tasks that support and sustain the change after project launch

When asked to do something new, people often have predictable attitudes and feelings. These reactions may be negative, and they can get in the way of successful implementation of all the project's benefits. Here are ways to plan for and cope with these reactions.

Effect of Change	Technique to Cope with this Reaction
People feel awkward, ill-at-ease, and self-conscious.	Acknowledge that this reaction is normal and temporary.
People think about what they will have to give up.	Help them understand the benefits of the change.
People feel alone even if everyone else is going through the change.	Assign mentors or partners in moving through the change.
People can handle only so much change. (Some can handle more than others.)	Provide tips on how to cope with change. Remind them that things get easier with time.
People are at different levels of readiness for change. (Some welcome it, and others are negative and cynical.)	Schedule brainstorming and problem-solving meetings to find creative ways to deal with the changes.
People believe that they don't have enough resources. (Sometimes this perception is not valid or accurate.)	Make sure there are enough resources and understand that some current activities may or definitely will go away. Use data to demonstrate that there are adequate resources.
People revert to their old behaviors or methods when the pressure is off.	Continue to maintain the gain. Use metrics to demonstrate and celebrate the benefits of the new methods, systems, or deliverables.
People impose boundaries and limitations on them-selves, sometimes without realizing it.	Communicate the constraints, if any, and actively remind people of the things they *can* do.
People don't always ask questions. (They make assumptions and act on them without checking.)	Hold periodic "town meetings" and Q&A sessions, or publish frequently asked questions (FAQs)

The Advanced Project Management Memory Jogger™

Don't forget to explain "What's In It For Me?" (WIIFM), to help people accept the changes and move forward.

3. Be creative in using other techniques for dealing with change.
   - Consider implementing the change in small steps or increments.
   - Design the new product or service to be compatible with the current deliverable. Use a familiar look and feel.
   - Identify someone who is credible and familiar to team members, and have him explain and "sell" the deliverable.
   - Make sure that the new product or service works right the first time and that it is reliable.
   - Offer small, simple, easy-to-try samples, trials, or previews.
   - If the new deliverable is not mandatory, provide a painless way to revert to the former deliverable or system if the deliverable does not work.

4. Coordinate the plan for organizational change with the project communication plan.
   - Identify any deliverables and the person accountable for each.
   - Involve the process owner(s) in the plan and implementation.
   - Monitor.
   - Develop survey and feedback tools to measure the success of the implementation.

Assemble the Project Management Plan

Once the team has completed the activities needed to produce a project management plan, it's time to assemble the plan and get it approved. The plan describes how the project will be executed to meet the project objectives. The plan should include an executive summary and all the documents, tables, lists, and so on that have been produced. Review the plan with the project sponsor and project customer, get it approved, and then distribute it.

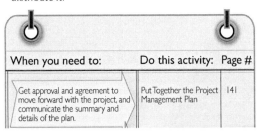

When you need to:	Do this activity:	Page #
Get approval and agreement to move forward with the project, and communicate the summary and details of the plan.	Put Together the Project Management Plan	141

Put Together the Project Management Plan

Why do it?

To create a document that details the project plan and describes how the project objectives can be met. After the plan is approved, it provides the road map for executing the project. The project management plan should be shared with project team members, stakeholders, the project manager, the project sponsor, and the project customer.

Project Management Plan
Leadership Summary

PROJECT SCOPE

- List the name and objective of the project.

- Describe the deliverables to be produced by the project, the life-cycle stages of each final deliverable, and the customer's criteria for accepting each final deliverable.

- List any organizational goals for the project.

 Don't forget about any organizational deliverables that are required by your project. Describe them and include acceptance criteria.

PROJECT RISK

- Summarize the key risk events, and determine the risk responses selected by the team to reduce the risk of not meeting project objectives.

PROJECT RESOURCES

Team membership: List the regular and ad hoc members of the team.

Schedule: Show the milestone schedule and the deadline dates. Define the team's risk rating for meeting the deadline dates and list the key countermeasures selected by the team to reduce the risk of not meeting the deadline dates.

Effort: List the estimate for the total staff time required for the project, including the accuracy rating for the estimate. Indicate the staffing limit, (if there is one), whether the estimate exceeds the limit, and if it does, the reason(s) why the estimate exceeds the limit.

Budget: List the total estimate for internal and external costs, and the total estimate for the project. Indicate the spending limit (if there is one), whether the estimate exceeds the limit, and if it does, the reasons) why the estimate exceeds the limit.

OTHER RESOURCES

- List any other key issues, including those related to project boundaries.

How do I do it?

1. Create an executive or leadership summary for the project management plan.

   ○ The summary's components and organization will vary according to your team's project and preferences, but you may want to use the outline on the previous page to get started.

2. Assemble the project management plan.

   ○ Include the following sections:

      ○ Original charter
      ○ Project scope
      ○ Project risk analysis
      ○ Project quality plan
      ○ Project procurement plan
      ○ List of required project status reports
      ○ Team membership of the project team
      ○ Project schedule(s)
      ○ Project contingency plan
      ○ Effort estimates and forecast (if required)
      ○ Budget estimates and forecast (if required)
      ○ Communication plan
      ○ Plan for dealing with organizational change

   ○ Attach tables, charts, and other diagrams as appropriate.

 The project management plan should be periodically updated as changes are approved.

3. Review the project management plan.

   ○ The core team members of the project (subproject leaders) should be involved in finalizing and reviewing the plan.

❍ Make sure the plan is reasonably complete and accurate considering the size and importance of the project.

4. Review the plan with the sponsor and customer, if appropriate.
   ❍ Make revisions to the final plan as needed, based on sponsor and customer input.

If you have involved the right people and been proactive about getting the information you need to plan the project, there should be very little change at this point.

5. Distribute the approved project management plan and the leadership summary.
   ❍ The project team members, project manager, project sponsor, and project customer should review, understand, and agree with the project management plan.
   ❍ Distribute the project management plan to these people, and the leadership summary to key stakeholders of the project.

The project management plan will be updated during execution, as needed to reflect agreed-upon changes to the plan and to the project. If the plan is not revised when changes are made, it will not be an effective tool to help you navigate execution of your project.

Chapter
FIVE

How to Execute the Project

Now that the project management plan has been completed and approved, it's time to *execute* the plan: create the deliverables according to the acceptance criteria, within the budget, and within the time schedule. As the project team executes the plan, team members will meet regularly to track their progress. In addition, you need to anticipate potential problems and address requests for changes to the project management plan. You also need

When you need to:	Do this activity:	Page #
Track and report the progress of the execution of the project	Monitor, Control, and Report Project Progress	146
Deal with problems or make changes to the project management plan	Resolve Problems and Manage Change	153
Review the progress of the project with the project sponsor and customer	Conduct Sponsor and Customer Reviews	159

to keep the project customer and the sponsor up-to-date through regularly scheduled review meetings.

Monitor, Control, and Report Project Progress

Why do it?

To ensure that the project is moving forward as planned and to gather information to feed into status reports. Monitoring the project's progress gives the project team a warning when things aren't going according to plan. In this way, the team can resolve problems and avoid more costly changes later.

How do I do it?

1. Determine how often the details of the project management plan should be monitored and compared to the actual results of the following project components:

   ○ Completion dates of deliverables

   ○ Effort (number of hours)

   ○ Expenditures (amount of money)

CASE STUDY

Amy Lee holds bi-monthly review meetings with the conference team during the early execution phase of the project. However, when the conference draws closer, the project team will meet weekly, or even daily if needed.

Monitoring and Controlling

How often you monitor your project depends on its length, size, speed, complexity, risk, and importance to the organization. Monitor subprojects at least as often as the main project—maybe more often.

Typically, the project manager and core team monitor the main project, and subproject leaders and their teams monitor the subprojects

You may want to monitor high-risk areas daily, particularly deliveries from vendors and items on the critical path. Refer to Critical Path, Chapter 4.

2. Assess the current status of the project.

   ○ Project team members provide updates on the status of their assignments and any work in their subprojects to their subproject leaders, who prepare their subproject status updates or reports before the project team assesses its status and progress.

   ○ If an agenda item for a project team review meeting might affect an ad hoc member, or if his viewpoint is needed to resolve an issue, be sure to invite him to participate.

3. Review the progress of the deliverables.

   ○ Were reviews as expected?

   ○ Were acceptance criteria met?

   ○ Any issues or concerns?

4. Compare the schedule, effort, and budget actuals to the project management plan, and identify any differences.

  ○ When the actual project results for cost and schedule differ from the plan, you need to know the reason for any difference, whether positive or negative.

If your team completed effort and spending forecasts as part of the project management plan, monitor these forecasts according to the time periods you defined. This practice will help you with earned value management if you are using it on your project. These forecasts also make it easy to calculate cost differences. Compare the forecast to the amount spent in light of the completed deliverables. If earned value management is not being used, then the project team and project manager will use their judgment to determine whether the difference is a problem and how significant it is.

Earned value management is an objective way to measure project performance and progress by comparing (a) the budgeted cost of the work performed to (b) the actual cost of the work performed.

For more on earned value management see *The Advanced Project Management Memory Jogger*™

Planned Value and Earned Value

The *planned value* (PV) is the monetary value you expect (plan) to earn at a given point in time. *Earned value* (EV) is the monetary value you actually earn at a given point in time. (Amounts shown below are in US dollars)

For example, if you plan to paint 40 houses in a sub-division and are to be paid $80,000 for the job, you can equate each house you paint as worth $2000. Your schedule shows that you expect to complete 10 houses per week. This equals $20,000 of planned value per week. If, at the end of the second week, you have only 18 houses painted (instead of the expected 20 houses), your earned value is $36,000, compared to your planned value of $40,000.

Earned value can also differ from the plan. For example, let's say you have a deliverable that was supposed to take two weeks and cost $300. But at the end of the first week you have accomplished 33% of the work. No matter what you have spent, you have earned $100 worth of value.

The Advanced Project Management Memory Jogger™

❍ All projects should measure completion dates, actual effort, and actual costs against the project plan. Some large, complex projects benefit from a more sophisticated measurement system that highlights spending that is too high for the completed work or insufficient progress for the amount actually spent.

❍ The project manager and project team must understand clearly why the results differ from the plan. If you do not know why, then the validity of the plan is in question. In the case study, Amy Lee was out of the office, and this is why the final program was late. Knowing *why* allows you to determine how to respond to the problem.

5. Decide what action should be taken, based on the difference(s).

❍ If there is no difference in the schedule, effort, or spending, and if the numbers are accurate, then the project is likely on course.

❍ If the difference is positive, you still need to understand the reason for it.

❍ If the difference is negative, you need to take further action. Do you know the reason for the difference? Is it a cause for concern? If the difference:

❍ Is not a cause for concern, simply report an explanation for the difference.

❍ Is a cause for concern and can be resolved easily (without changes to the project management plan), then resolve it.

❍ Cannot be resolved easily, put it on the issues list, along with the date required for its resolution.

❍ If the action to resolve the difference requires changes to the project management plan, use the flowchart on page 158 as a guide in making

Differences from the Project Management Plan for the 3-Day Conference

Project Plan Area	Project Plan (including changes)	Actual Project Results	Difference	Reason
Schedule (completion dates)				
Issue Final Program	5/1	5/4	3 days late	Amy Lee was out sick for a week, which delayed the program.
Complete Review for Preliminary Brochure	5/18	5/20	2 days late	The delay in issuing the program created a delay in completing the brochure.
Effort				
Cumulative Hours Expended	985 hours	1075 hours	90 hours over	Preparation of the marketing materials took longer than projected.
Cost				
Internal Charges	N/A	N/A	N/A	N/A
Cumulative External Charges	$29,450	$28,950	$500 under	Hotel deposit was $500 less than planned.

changes. The activity "Resolve Problems and Manage Change" on pages 153–158 describes the process for making changes.

Being ahead of schedule or under budget is usually good, but it indicates that the project has deviated from the project management plan. Perhaps something is missing or a problem exists that could later produce negative effects. Examine the reasons for every difference, whether positive or negative. If you discover the potential for future problems, perform a risk analysis and develop risk responses to eliminate or reduce the probability that these problems can occur.

6. Review actual and anticipated problems and requests for changes to the project management plan.

   ○ If requests for changes have been made, follow your team's process for managing change (see page 158 for a sample process).

   ○ Scan the environment for potential problems: organizational, regulatory, competitive, and technological changes that may have an impact on the project.

Actively monitor the customer's situation for changes. Customers may not notify you of a change in their situation, not realizing that it can affect the project.

7. Whether on the phone, in a face-to-face meeting or on a webinar, clear the parking lot, and review and update the issues list.

   ○ Review the parking lot to be sure that all the issues, ideas, or questions that were brought up during the project status review have been addressed.

○ Review all the issues on the issues list, and update the status of each one.

○ If the team cannot resolve an issue or cannot resolve it by the required date, decide what further action is required, and discuss with your sponsor if appropriate.

8. Recognize accomplishments in the project, and evaluate the project status review process.

○ See "Evaluate Your Meetings," Chapter 3, page 49.

○ Focus on team members' accomplishments, and obtain feedback.

Resolve Problems and Manage Change

Why do it?

To respond to problems or requests for changes to the project management plan. Having a process for managing changes gives the team a way of revising the plan when needed so that the project stays focused on satisfying the customer. It also prevents scope creep—the subtle, often unnoticed expansion of the project's scope as it is executed.

How do I do it?

1. When a change is proposed, decide whether it is a good idea.

○ Requests for changes may come from someone outside the team, such as the project sponsor or customer. As the project environment changes, you may need to make changes to the project management plan to address the new situation.

○ Not every proposed change should be adopted.

Be sure to ask, "Is this change good for the customer? The organization? The project?"

○ If the change is not a good idea or will not add value to the project, put it on the issues list to resolve with the person who requested the change.

2. If the change is a good idea and doesn't modify the intent of the project management plan, then revise the project management plan to clarify.

3. If the change requires modifying the intent of the project management plan, then define the impact on the plan and prepare a change request.

○ A *change request* is a one-page description of the proposed change and its impact on the project. It should explain how the change will affect the project's risk level, scope, effort, cost, or schedule.

○ Most parts of the project management plan are interdependent, meaning that if one part is changed, other parts will likely need to be changed. For example, if a change to the project scope is required, it will probably affect the schedule, effort, budget, and risks of creating the deliverables. Be sure to examine the impact of the proposed change to make sure that it won't cause unintended consequences.

A change to the project management plan should follow the same steps as creating the original project management plan. If the change is simple, the team can go through the steps quickly. The project decision criteria (from the project charter) can guide the process. For example, if the schedule is most important and a change has been requested to the scope of the project, look for ways to change the effort and budget before extending the schedule.

Amy Lee found out that the organization's print shop was having equipment problems that would delay the conference proceedings.

Project Change Request for 3-Day Conference

Date: July 10th	Originator: Amy Lee Request #: 15
Description of change:	Go to an outside printer to print conference proceedings.
Reason for change:	Print Shop equipment has a lot of down time, the projected workload in August is high.
Proposed solution:	Obtain bids and outsource printing.
Impact on scope:	None if approved
Impact on risk:	None if approved
Impact on cost:	$500 increase
Impact on schedule:	None if approved

Comments:

Approvals:	Project Manager	Project Sponsor	Project Customer
Signature:	Amy Lee	Chris Wheeler	Chris Wheeler
Date approved:	July 12	July 14	July 14

Five Common Reasons
for a Change in a Project's Scope

1. **Errors in defining the deliverables,** including missing, unnecessary, or inaccurate deliverables.

2. **Errors in defining the project.** The deliverables are correct, but the project itself was incorrectly defined.

3. **Customer or stakeholder requests.** It's best to minimize unnecessary changes in project scope. Early in the project, you should define and publish the criteria and the timeline for accepting discretionary changes in the project scope.

4. **Value-added changes.** For example, a team member may find a better, faster, less-expensive way to do the work and still meet the project objectives.

5. **External events.** These changes in the environment are outside the project manager's control but must be accommodated.

The Advanced Project Management Memory Jogger™

4. Have the change request approved, and implement the change.
   - ○ Usually the project manager and the sponsor approve the change request.
   - ○ The customer should also approve the change request as appropriate.
5. Update the project management plan to incorporate the change.
   - ○ The project manager is responsible for incorporating the change by amending the appropriate parts of the project management plan.

5 | Execute the Project 157

Managing Project Change

The following flow chart shows the steps involved in managing change in a project.

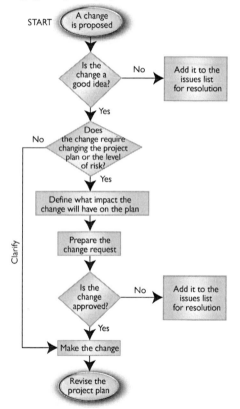

Conduct Sponsor and Customer Reviews

Why do it?

To periodically review the progress of the project with the sponsor or the customer (or both) to keep them informed and to obtain their support, advice, help, and confidence.

How do I do it?

1. Hold periodic project sponsor and customer meetings to review the status of the project.

   ○ If the project team meets, for example, once per week, then schedule a review with the project customer or sponsor once per month.

   ○ Routine meetings with the sponsor and customer are usually held less often than project team meetings, depending on the length of the project, the level of activity, and the degree of project risk.

   ○ Informal, informational update meetings between the project manager and the project sponsor or customer should be held as needed.

   ○ Whenever a critical issue or serious problem arises, the project manager should involve the project customer or sponsor *immediately* as appropriate.

 Check to see whether you can combine the sponsor and customer review meetings. This practice will save time for everyone involved in the meetings.

For many internal projects, the project sponsor is also the project customer. When the project customer is from another department or organization, the sponsor may be the primary contact.

2. Review the current status of the project.

   ○ The project manager reports on the progress of the deliverables, and the status of the schedule, effort, budget, and risk.

3. Discuss changes in the environment and anticipated problems that could affect the project.

   ○ Review potential problems and changes to the project management plan. The customer and sponsor may provide information on the project environment and suggestions for resolving problems.

4. Review the issues list.

   ○ Review the status of the issues that are external to the team and that require the involvement or assistance of the project sponsor. Also make sure that the sponsor is informed of any issues that could be a future problem.

Remember—no surprises! It's a good career strategy. Before issues with other areas are published in your project status report, get the approval of the project sponsor.

○ The project customer and sponsor do not need to be involved with issues that will be resolved within the team, but they do need to be informed of the issues that may affect them or that require their assistance or intervention.

Be sure that the project team has exhausted its options for resolving a problem before asking the project sponsor or customer to get involved—unless a simple answer from one of them could resolve the issue quickly.

5. Solicit feedback from the project sponsor and customer on ways to improve the project.

○ Ask for feedback and solicit ideas, including political advice, for improving the project.

Keep the project sponsor and customer involved and interested in your project by communicating with them often. This practice increases their confidence in the team and enhances the team's credibility.

6

Close Ou
- Evaluate the
- Prepare closeo

Chapter
SIX

How to Close Out the Project

When the project customer accepts the final deliverable, it's time to close out the project. A project is closed out when you complete the *closeout report* and the project sponsor has accepted it. This report encompasses the final project status report, customer and sponsor feedback, lessons learned, and recommendations for improvement.

When you need to:	Do this activity:	Page #
Obtain feedback from the project sponsor and customer about the project's deliverables and process	Survey the Project Customer's and Sponsor's Satisfaction and Feedback	164
Translate feedback and analysis of the project into useful information for future projects	Develop Lessons Learned	167
Complete the project	Create the Closeout Report	171

Survey the Project Sponsor's and Customer's Satisfaction and Feedback

Why do it?

To solicit feedback and ideas for improvement from the project sponsor and customer. This feedback covers the project process as well as final project results. You will use this information to develop the lessons learned and to write the project closeout report.

How do I do it?

1. Review the final project metrics.
   - Review the final project management plan, and prepare the final project status report. (*see next page*)

In the section of the report, "Changes to Plan" the column labeled "Baseline" is the scope of the project management plan when it was first approved (before any scope changes occurred during the project). This section refers to the budget, delivery dates, and the amount of effort, usually in hours. List the planned deliverables and the approved changes to the deliverables; insert a short summary of how the deliverables were modified and approved during project execution as needed. For more, see *The Advanced Project Management Memory Jogger™*

2. Solicit the project customer's and sponsor's satisfaction and feedback regarding the final deliverables and the project process. (See survey on page 166.)
   - Record this information on the satisfaction feedback survey form.
   - Ask for comments or suggestions for improvement.

3. Total and average the survey responses, and share them with the team.
   - The survey will also be part of the closeout report.

FINAL PROJECT STATUS REPORT

Date: _____
Project Name: _____   Project Number: _____
Project Manager: _____   Project Sponsor: _____

Scope Status

Final Deliverable(s)	Acceptance Criteria	Criteria Met/Comment

Schedule Status

Final Deliverable(s) & Key Milestones	Approved Dates	Actual Completion Dates

Effort and Spending Status

	Approved Amounts	Actual Amounts
Effort (Hours)		
Spending (Money)		

Changes to Plan (Total Changes)

	Baseline	Approved Changes	Final Approved Amounts
Deliverable(s)			
Deadline			
Effort			
Spending			

Explain all differences:

SATISFACTION FEEDBACK SURVEY

Project Objectives

(Please circle one number for each question.)	Strongly Disagree			Strongly Agree		
1. Final deliverables met the acceptance criteria	1	2	3	4	5	6
2. Delivery dates met the approved schedule	1	2	3	4	5	6
3. Final cost was within approved budget	1	2	3	4	5	6

Comments:

Project Process Results

(Please circle one number for each question.)	Strongly Disagree			Strongly Agree		
4. Project management plan was complete and worked well.	1	2	3	4	5	6
5. Management/Sponsor supported the project.	1	2	3	4	5	6
6. The change management process was effective.	1	2	3	4	5	6
7. Status reports were clear and complete.	1	2	3	4	5	6
8. Customer input and review meetings were effective.	1	2	3	4	5	6
9. Project team kept the sponsor and customer informed.	1	2	3	4	5	6
10. Project communication was complete, adequate, and clear.	1	2	3	4	5	6

Comments:

Suggestions for improvement:

When possible, have a conversation about this feedback. <u>Meet with the customer and sponsor in person or by phone.</u> (Sending the survey by e-mail is not as effective, but if you send it, make sure to get it back.) The objective is to learn as much as possible, and the best way to do that is to listen with the intent to understand. Listen to what they have to say without being defensive. Ask clarifying questions if needed.

 To measure progress and determine trends, use the same feedback form/questions for all your projects.

Develop Lessons Learned

Why do it?

<u>To review the project's results and translate them into lessons learned and recommendations for improvement.</u> This document will benefit the organization by providing these lessons to future projects. Include the project team and others—project customer, sponsor, and major stakeholders—as appropriate.

How do I do it?

1. Review the actual project results and compare to the final project management plan in the relevant areas.

   ○ Review the project charter, project management plan, final status report, and satisfaction feedback survey. Were all the project objectives met?

   ○ Analyze the entire issues list for the duration of the project. Were all the issues resolved? Can you derive any significant trends, problems, and insights from the issues? Are a disproportionate number from one or two areas or phases of the project?

   ○ Evaluate the deliverables. Were they completed per the approved acceptance criteria? Were the criteria accurate and adequate? Did the reviews ensure the quality of the deliverables?

   ○ Review the project boundaries analysis. Did you miss related projects and initiatives?

   ○ Examine the risk analysis reports for the acceptance criteria, deadlines, and budget limits. How well did the team predict and mitigate risks? Did the risk responses work well?

   ○ Assess the team membership. Did you have all the needed skills and resources? Were the right people on the team? Were the liaison and ad hoc members valuable? Quantify the effects and impact of the team membership.

   ○ Study all change requests, whether approved or not approved. Did you fail to document or get approval for any changes made?

   ○ Review any deviations from the plan (schedule, cost, effort, etc.). Why did the differences occur—wrong estimates, poor performance, other reasons? If the causes aren't understood, further analysis may be needed. Could the differences have been avoided?

- ○ Were the procurement and quality plans (where applicable) effective and complete?
- ○ Review project contingency to determine whether the amounts were reasonable and adequate.
- ○ Survey the audiences for your project communication and status reports to determine whether the communication plan was complete and effective.
- ○ Discuss support for the project from the management of the organization. Was it adequate? Why or why not?
- ○ Evaluate the project team meetings. (See Chapter 3) Were they efficient and effective? What could be improved? Look for trends in the scores and comments over time: did they get better? How?

 For complex projects, each subproject team should develop its own lessons learned and then share them with the larger project team. The project team should concentrate on lessons learned from the project as a whole.

2. Discuss the lessons learned on the project, and develop ideas for improvement. Be sure to note successes as well as problems.
- ○ Discuss lessons learned for each area of the project: deliverables, reviews and approvals, team membership, and so on.
- ○ What can be improved in each of these project areas so that future teams can duplicate the same successes and avoid making the same mistakes?

LESSONS LEARNED RECOMMENDATIONS

Date: _____
Project Name: _____   Project Number: _____
Project Manager: _____   Project Sponsor: _____

Project Objectives	Worked /Continue	Didn't Work/Modify
Scope		
Schedule		
Cost		
Effort		
Project Area	**Worked /Continue**	**Didn't Work/Modify**
Project Initiation		
Project Management Plan		
Project Execution		
Project Closeout		
Communication Plan		
Team Membership		
Risk Analysis		
Quality Plan		
Procurement Plan		
Project Change Management Plan		
Recommendations:		

Create the Closeout Report

Why do it?

To complete a report for the organization that describes the performance of the project, contains lessons learned, and makes recommendations to senior management for improvements in the project management process. By preparing a closeout report, the team shares its project experiences to support continuous improvement in the organization.

How do I do it?

1. Create an executive summary of the closeout report.

   - Prepare a short narrative of the key findings from the final project results.

   - Include a section for each area listed in the lessons learned document. Describe what was learned in each area and what should be done differently next time.

   - In the lessons learned section, summarize the overall lessons learned from the project and recommendations for improvement.

2. Attach the final project status report; feedback from the project customer, sponsor, and team; lessons learned; and recommendations for future projects, if available.

   - Record the feedback received from the project customer, sponsor, and team members. Include any results from review meetings.

3. Obtain the approval of the sponsor.

   - Review the project management plan, satisfaction feedback survey, final status report, lessons learned, and any change requests with the sponsor and customer, if appropriate.

○ Discuss ideas for improvement. Review the team's recommendations for improvement, and solicit additional ideas from the project sponsor.

4. Distribute and archive the closeout report.

○ Provide a copy of the report to the project sponsor and the team, other project managers and the project office or project steering group. The report will serve as a source of ideas for improvement and as data for an organization-wide view of projects.

If there is not already a central repository of closeout reports for your organization or area, create one. If possible, use a search engine and key words to allow others to take full advantage of the information contained in the reports.

CASE STUDY

Closeout Report for the 3-Day Conference

Executive Summary of the Project

Project Scope and Risk

The 3-day conference had a variety of topics, top-notch speakers, and networking opportunities. The conference met requirements because the participants rated the sessions at 4.3. The goal was 4.0. Participants and customers said the location was good, but the meeting rooms were not always adequate. The presentations were satisfactory, and the topics were rated above average.

The main risk, not getting enough high-quality speakers, was avoided by offering to publish the speakers' papers in a monthly magazine.

Schedule
Plan date for the conference: September 27–29
Actual date for the conference: September 27–29

Continued...

The schedule was adequate and allowed enough time to secure the speakers and the hotel. At least six months is needed for these activities. The brochure and postcard were sent out early enough and generated 325 registrations. The organizational goal was 300 registrations.

Effort

Total effort in plan: 1,375 hours or about 8 months (medium accuracy)
Changes made to plan: None
Actual effort time: 1,625 hours or about 9 1/2 months

The actual effort time was within the range projected in the plan (1,030 to 1,720 hours). Most of the deviation from the plan was within the Marketing subproject.

Costs

Total external costs in plan: $85,400 (high accuracy)
Changes made to plan: $500 or more for outside printing
Actual external costs: $84,775

The budget and subsequent changes were adequate to stay within budget limits. The food did not receive high ratings, so the allowance for food should be increased next year. Maintain the marketing budget to purchase additional mailing lists. The original budget and subsequent change orders were reasonable.

Lessons Learned

Successes

Deliverables

- Conference location (warm location was a plus)
- Conference size (good size but could be as large as 400)
- Choice of speakers and speaker presentations
  (excellent balance of consultants and practitioners)

Project process

- Project plan (helpful because the team knew when to do what)

Continued...

Recommendations for improvement

Deliverables

- Hotel food needs more variety and healthier options
- Meeting rooms should be larger with more open space

Project Process

- More complete information in the charter will reduce rework; constraints not always known until work was done
- Better risk assessment will reduce rework and inefficiencies.

Attachment

- Participant Feedback and Customer Satisfaction Surveys
- Final Project Status Report

In Closing

Thank you for investing in your capabilities and career by reading the second edition of *The Project Management Memory Jogger*. We hope you found many useful best practices, tips and ideas for more successful projects, and that you now have a better understanding of project management. In addition, you will find that your ability to navigate project issues and politics and to successfully negotiate resources and support for your projects has improved.

By learning to quantify and communicate options, using the language of management—time, money, and quality—your projects will be more successful. We welcome your comments and suggestions. Please contact Karen Tate at ktate@griffintate.com.

Appendix A

Deliverable Life Cycle Stages

A deliverable is a product, service, or process. Deliverables have life cycles composed of the stages of development. Humans also have a life cycle - birth, childhood, adolescence, adulthood, middle age, old age, & death. Think "cradle to grave."

Why do it?

To define the start and end points of the project's involvement to create the final deliverable in order to further clarify the project scope.

How do I do it?

1. Determine the life-cycle stages (LCS) which the project team will start and end the work on the final deliverable(s). Every product, service, or process has life-cycle stages.

   o The table on page 178 shows 6 typical generic life-cycle stages in the development of any product, service, or process.

 Define life-cycle stage boundaries for each major final and organizational deliverable.

2. Verify the stages that are part of, and are the responsibility of the project. Since the life-cycle stages are independent of the project, it is important for the project team to determine these and obtain approval from the sponsor and/or customer.

3. Develop a "tollgate" or acceptance criteria at the end of the each life-cycle stage to ensure the interim deliverables meet the criteria to move forward.

Some projects will have financial performance tollgates based on the current financial projections of the project costs and benefits.

During each LCS, there is one or more interim or final deliverables. Performing the life-cycle stage analysis provides a preliminary list of interim deliverables in chronological order, and helps make sense of the flow of the work early in the project.

Generic Life Cycle Stages for a Product, Service, or Process Deliverable

Life-Cycle Stage	Typical Terms for Stage of Development	Generic Description of Stage Activities
1	Concept	• Define the problem or opportunity
	Definition	• Define the deliverable and characteristics
Tollgate		
2	Design	• Detail the features and functions
	Planning	• Finalize requirements
		• Determine interim and final deliverables, acceptance criteria
Tollgate		
3	Acquisition	• Train
	Development	• Pilot test, prototype
	Construction	• Fabricate, build
	Installation	• Assemble, set-up
Tollgate		
4	Verification	• Launch
	Qualification	• Implement
	Go live, start-up	• Test
	Implementation	• Inspect
		• Hand over to operations owner

Tollgate		
5	Operations & maintenance	• Use deliverable
		• Follow process
		• Provide service
		• Produce and deliver product

Tollgate		
6	Retire	• Return resources (people, equipment, matls.)
		• Dismantle equipment
		• Dispose, recycle, or reuse materials.

Software Life Cycle Stages Example (Waterfall Model)

Software development is a common use of LCS. There are many variations of software development models with different and more or fewer stages

Life-Cycle Stage	Stage of Development	Description of Stage Activities
1	Analysis	• Determine what needs to be done
2	Design	• Finalize requirements
		• Functional & Technical Specifications
3	Develop, test	• Coding & testing
4	Implementation	• Go live
		• User Acceptance Test
		• Transfer to operations owner
5	Operation & maintenance	• Use software and maintain
6	Retire	• Retire the software application

There can be more or fewer stages, depending on the deliverable.

Life Cycle Stages for Six Sigma DMAIC Projects

DMAIC Six Sigma Projects should be planned as two projects or in two stages, because in the beginning, the root cause is not yet known, and a solution cannot be developed and planned until you have completed the "analyze" phase.

Life-Cycle Stage	Typical Terms for Stage of Development	Description of Stage Activities
1	Define	• Determine what to measure
2	Measure	• Gather data
3	Analyze	• Determine root cause, define the solution

Begin planning and estimating the implementation and control stages after the solution has been defined and approved

4	Implement	• Develop solution and implement
5	Control	• Operate, monitor and verify results
		• Standardize process

Life-Cycle Stages and Interim Deliverables for the 3-Day Conference

The table on the next two pages show the life-cycle stages, activities, and some of the interim deliverables for the 3-day conference. The generic activities in the table that did not fit the conference were deleted.

Life-Cycle Stages for the 3-Day Conference

Life Cycle Stage	Stage of Development	Stage Activities	Interim Deliverables
1	Concept and definition	Define the problem or opportunity that the conference will address. Define the characteristics of the conference.	• Preliminary program
2	Develop and design	Plan and document the interim and the final deliverables. Review the plan.	• Hotel contract • Speaker contracts • Final program • Conference plan and schedule (setup, workers, layout of facilities, room assignments, registration, tear'down)
3	Prepare and install	Train people. Set up or install equipment.	• Speaker instructions • Trained conference workers continued...

Note: The conference boundaries are the beginning of LCS 1 and the end of LCS 6.

Continued... Life-Cycle Stages for the 3-Day Conference

Life Cycle Stage	Stage of Development	Stage Activities	Interim Deliverables
4	Verify and test	Pilot test. Pre-start up. Hand over operations.	• Equipment set up • Approved checklist • Sign-off
5	Operations and maintenance	Implement the plan fully. Provide service to customer.	• Conference proceedings • Audiotapes of sessions • Hold conference
6	Retire	Return resources (people, equipment, and materials) to the organization. Dismantle equipment. Dispose, recycle, or reuse materials.	• Equipment breakdown and return • Conference materials returned to stock or recycled. • Participants and speakers go back to their jobs

Create an Activity Schedule

Why do it?

To create a schedule of the activities required to create all of the interim and final deliverables. The activity schedule shows how each activity can be completed at the appropriate time, ensuring that the final deliverable will be completed on time.

How do I do it?

1. Create a diagram on flip chart paper that will show the flow of all the activities that need to be completed for the project.

   ○ To begin constructing the activity schedule, take 3-4 pieces of flip chart paper, at least 10 feet long, and tape it to a wall or long table.

   ○ Draw or tape a copy of the milestone schedule along the bottom of the paper to create a schedule timeline. (See Chapter 4, for instructions on how to create a milestone schedule.)

   ○ On both ends of the timeline, draw a vertical line.

   ○ On the outside of the left vertical line, write the names of the people who will be responsible for getting the activities of the subproject completed. Leave enough space to fit all the sticky notes of activities next to each name.

   ○ Separate the names of team members from the non-team members.

   ○ Draw a horizontal line across the diagram. This line should be above all the names of team members and non-team members and should extend from one end of the diagram to the other.

   ○ Above the horizontal line, and to the right of the right vertical line, list the deliverables for either the project or the subproject, depending on the complexity of the project.

> – For simple projects (this schedule is optional): The project team should list the final deliverables and organizational deliverables for the project.

> – For complex projects: The subproject team should list the final deliverables and the organizational deliverables for the subproject, or tape a copy of the part of the WBS diagram that is specific to the subproject.

If a subproject team is creating its own activity schedule, add the subproject team's milestone dates to the project's milestone dates listed along the timeline.

2. Identify all the activities that must be accomplished to create each interim and final deliverable.

   ○ Write each activity on a sticky note. Leave space on the sticky notes to write the name of the person who is responsible for the activity, and space for the start and end date of the activity.

   ○ One way to identify activities is to refer to the arrows on the deliverables schedule. These arrows represent the activities required to transform a deliverable into the next deliverable in the sequence, ending with the final deliverable. If the team translates each arrow into an activity or set of activities, all of the activities for each final deliverable will be captured, in the order in which they will occur.

   ○ In the space above the horizontal line of the diagram, line up the activities needed to create each deliverable with the appropriate final deliverable or subproject listed on the right hand side of the diagram. Sequence the order of activities from left to right on the diagram.

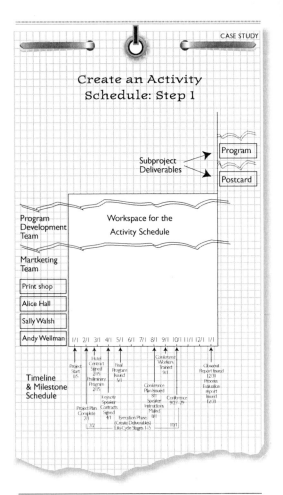

Create an Activity
Schedule: Step 1

Subproject
Deliverables

Program

Postcard

Program
Development
Team

Workspace for the
Activity Schedule

Martketing
Team

Print shop

Alice Hall

Sally Walsh

Andy Wellman

1/1 2/1 3/1 4/1 5/1 6/1 7/1 8/1 9/1 10/1 11/1 12/1 1/1

Timeline
& Milestone
Schedule

Project
Start
1/5

Hotel
Contract
Signed
2/15
Preliminary
Program
2/15

Final
Program
Issued
5/1

Conference
Workers
Trained
9/1

Conference
Plan Issued
8/1

Closeout
Report Issued
12/31
Process
Evaluation
report
Issued
12/31

Keynote
Speaker
Contracts
Signed
4/1

Speaker
Instructions
Mailed
8/1

Conference
9/27-29

Project Plan
Complete
2/1
1/2/1

Execution Phase
(Create Deliverables)
Life-Cycle Stages 1-5
10/1

Be sure to include review activities and risk responses as sticky notes since these are also activities. To make it clear which activities belong with each final deliverable, where possible, use different colors sticky notes to see the flow of activities for any specific deliverable. Don't forget to create sticky notes for activities that will create the organizational deliverables.

3. Vertically align the activities so that they meet the delivery dates for the appropriate deliverable.

  ○ Use the delivery dates from the deliverables schedule.

  ○ Adjust the delivery dates, if necessary, to create a workable schedule that meets the deadlines.

  ○ After aligning all the activities, write the start date in the lower left corner of the sticky notes and put the end date in the lower right corner.

After all of the activities have been assigned a start and end date, the critical path can be calculated. (This is optional.) The critical path is the shortest possible path from the first activity to the last. Refer to *The Advanced Project Management Memory Jogger™*, for instructions on calculating the critical path.

If you adjust an activity end date, which then changes the team's delivery date for a deliverable, make sure the revised delivery date does not exceed the deadline date for the deliverable, if it has one. If the revised delivery date exceeds the deadline date, put this problem on the issues list and resolve it with the sponsor and/or the customer.

4. Move all the sticky notes below the horizontal line of the diagram, aligning each activity with the person who is responsible for completing it.

  ○ Move the sticky notes to align them with the name of the person who is responsible for completing the activity. Keep each sticky note aligned with the completion date for the activity.

○ Add the name of the person who is responsible for completing the activity to each sticky note.

 Make sure that you haven't assigned more work than each person can accomplish by the completion dates required. If you have, either reassign an activity or adjust the schedule.

5. Using arrows, connect one activity to the next activity in the chain.

○ In the deliverables schedule, the arrows represent activities. In the activity schedule, the arrows represent deliverables.

 Check the arrows to see if they represent deliverables (which they should) or activities (which they shouldn't). If any arrows actually represent activities, replace the arrow with a sticky note of the activity.

 If any of the arrows go outside the subproject, make sure the deliverable created as a result of this activity is included on the deliverables schedule.

6. Assign a coordinator to any activity that will be completed by someone outside the project team.

○ Assign someone from the team, (or in the case of subprojects, someone from the subproject team), who will be accountable for making sure the activity gets done.

○ Put the coordinator's name on the sticky note and mark it with a "C." This will remind the team that activities need to be coordinated and who is responsible for coordinating them.

7. For each review listed in the review and approvals table, add a start and end date in the table.

○ Creating a reviews and approvals table is described in the section called "Develop a Project Quality Plan" in Chapter 4.

8. Revisit the team's risk ratings for meeting the deadline dates for the final deliverables. Revise if necessary.

   ○ If the team's risk level is 4 or higher, define some countermeasures that will decrease the team's risk to at least a 3. If the team cannot lower its risk level to at least 3, add this to the issues list to resolve with the sponsor.

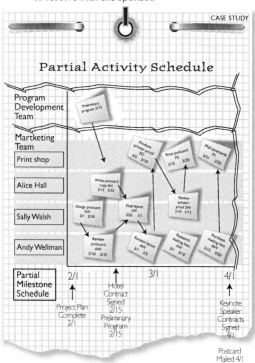

Partial Activity Schedule

Program Development Team
- Preliminary program 2/15

Marketing Team

Print shop
- Produce printer proof PD 3/5 3/10
- Print postcard PS 3/12 3/20
- Mail postcards PS 3/21 3/25

Alice Hall
- Write postcard copy AH 2/15 2/25

Sally Walsh
- Design postcard SW 2/1 2/10
- Final layout SW 2/25 3/1
- Review printer proof SW 3/10 3/12

Andy Wellman
- Review postcard AW 2/10 2/15
- Review layout AW 3/1 3/5
- Research mailing lists AW 3/1 3/10
- Purchase mailing lists AW 3/15 3/20

Partial Milestone Schedule

2/1 — Project Plan Complete 2/1

2/15 — Hotel Contract Signed 2/15 / Preliminary Program 2/15

3/1

4/1 — Keynote Speaker Contracts Signed 4/1

Postcard Mailed 4/1

Partial Activity Schedule

The illustration on the previous page shows some of the activities to be completed by the Marketing subproject team of the conference project to produce the postcard.

Draw a Gantt Chart

Why do it?

To display the major activities of the project and their duration. The Gantt chart helps both the team and people outside the team to understand the major activities of the project and their progression in time.

How do I do it?

1. Using the deliverables schedule, draw a bar around each deliverable that extends from the start date of the first activity to the date of the last activity.

   - ❍ The bar indicates the amount of time that it will take to complete all the activities that are needed to create the deliverable.

   - ❍ Inside the bar, write the name of the overall activity that the bar represents and the person who is accountable for making sure the deliverable gets created.

   - ❍ There will be one bar for each interim deliverable, which means there will be more than one bar in line with each branch of the tree diagram (or with each final deliverable listed on the outside of the left vertical line).

   - ❍ Remove the deliverables sticky notes from the schedule.

 Before you begin, make sure you've captured the deliverables schedule information.

Partial Gantt Chart of Activities for the 3-Day Conference Project

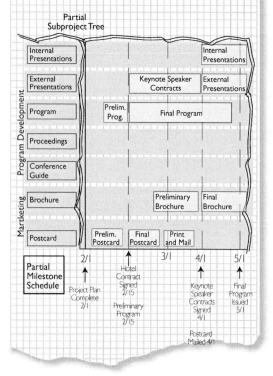

Partial Subproject Tree

Program Development
- Internal Presentations
- External Presentations
- Program — Prelim. Prog. / Final Program
- Proceedings
- Conference Guide

Marketing
- Brochure — Preliminary Brochure / Final Brochure
- Postcard — Prelim. Postcard / Final Postcard / Print and Mail

Keynote Speaker Contracts — External Presentations

Internal Presentations

Partial Milestone Schedule

2/1
3/1
4/1
5/1

Project Plan Complete 2/1

Hotel Contract Signed 2/15

Preliminary Program 2/15

Keynote Speaker Contracts Signed 4/1

Postcard Mailed 4/1

Final Program Issued 5/1

Appendix B

Additional Tools for Project Team Members

The following are three tools that are available for project teams to use in building consensus. Excerpted from, and for more tools like these, see *The Memory Jogger™ 2, 2nd edition.*

AFFINITY
DIAGRAM
Gathering & grouping ideas

Why use it?

To allow a team to creatively generate a large number of ideas/issues and then organize and summarize natural groupings among them to understand the essence of a problem and breakthrough solutions.

What does it do?

- Encourages creativity by everyone on the team at all phases of the process
- Breaks down long-standing communication barriers
- Encourages nontraditional connections among ideas/issues
- Allows breakthroughs to emerge naturally, even on long-standing issues
- Encourages "ownership" of results that emerge because the team creates both the detailed input and general results
- Overcomes "team paralysis," which is brought on by an overwhelming array of options and lack of consensus

How do I do it?

1. **Phrase the issue under discussion in a full sentence.**

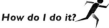

What are the issues involved in planning
fun family vacations?

2. **Brainstorm at least 20 ideas or issues.**

   a) Follow guidelines for brainstorming.

   b) Record each idea on a sticky note in bold, large print to make it visible 4–6 feet away. Use, at minimum, a noun and a verb. Avoid using single words. Four to seven words work well.

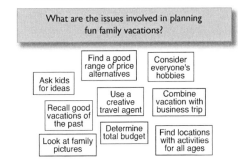

What are the issues involved in planning fun family vacations?

Find a good range of price alternatives

Consider everyone's hobbies

Ask kids for ideas

Use a creative travel agent

Combine vacation with business trip

Recall good vacations of the past

Determine total budget

Find locations with activities for all ages

Look at family pictures

Note: There are 10 to 40 more ideas in a typical Affinity Diagram

A "typical" Affinity has 40–60 items; it is not unusual to have 100–200 ideas.

3. **Without talking, sort ideas simultaneously into 5–10 related groupings.**

   a) Move sticky notes where they fit best for you. Don't ask; simply move any notes that you think belong in another grouping.

b) Sorting will slow down or stop when each person feels sufficiently comfortable with the groupings.

> **What are the issues involved in planning fun family vacations?**

Ask kids for ideas	Find a good range of price alternatives	Use a creative travel agent
Consider everyone's hobbies	Combine vacation with business trip	Find locations with activities for all ages
Look at family pictures	Determine total budget	Recall good vacations of the past

Note: There are usually 5 to 10 more groupings of ideas in a typical Affinity Diagram.

 Sort in silence to focus on the meaning behind and connections among all ideas, instead of emotions and "history" that often arise in discussions.

 As an idea is moved back and forth, try to see the logical connection that the other person is making. If this movement continues beyond a reasonable point, agree to create a duplicate sticky note.

 It is okay for some notes to stand alone. These "loners" can be as important as others that fit into groupings naturally.

4. **For each grouping, create summary or header cards using consensus.**

   a) Gain a quick team consensus on a word or phrase that captures the central idea/theme of each grouping; record it on a sticky note, and place it at the top of each grouping. These are draft header cards.

b) For each grouping, agree on a concise sentence that combines the grouping's central idea and what all of the specific sticky notes add to that idea; record it, and replace the draft version. This is a final header card.

c) Divide large groupings into subgroups as needed, and create appropriate subheaders.

d) Draw the final Affinity Diagram connecting all finalized header cards with their groupings.

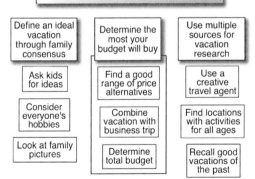

Note: There are usually 5 to 10 groupings of ideas in a typical Affinity. This is a partial Affinity.

Spend the extra time needed to do solid header cards. Strive to capture the essence of all of the ideas in each grouping. Shortcuts here can greatly reduce the effectiveness of the final Affinity Diagram.

 It is possible that a note within a grouping could become a header card. However, don't choose the "closest one" because it's convenient. The hard work of creating new header cards often leads to breakthrough ideas.

Variations

Another popular form of this tool, called the KJ Method, was developed by the Japanese anthropologist Jiro Kawakita while he was doing fieldwork in the 1950s. The KJ Method, identified with Kawakita's initials, helped the anthropologist and his students gather and analyze data. The KJ Method differs from the Affinity Diagram described above in that the cards are fact-based and go through a highly structured refinement process before the final diagram is created.

Affinity

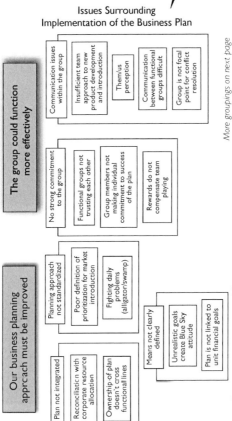

Issues Surrounding
Implementation of the Business Plan

The group could function more effectively

- Communication issues within the group
- Insufficient team approach to new product development and introduction
- Them/us perception
- Communication between functional groups difficult
- Group is not focal point for conflict resolution

- No strong commitment to the group
- Functional groups not trusting each other
- Group members not making individual commitment to success of the plan
- Rewards do not compensate team playing

More groupings on next page

Our business planning approach must be improved

- Planning approach not standardized
- Poor definition of prioritization for market introduction
- Fighting daily problems (alligator/swamp)

- Plan not integrated
- Reconciliation with corporate resource allocation
- Ownership of plan doesn't cross functional lines

- Means not clearly defined
- Unrealistic goals create Blue Sky attitude
- Plan is not linked to unit financial goals

Information provided courtesy of Goodyear

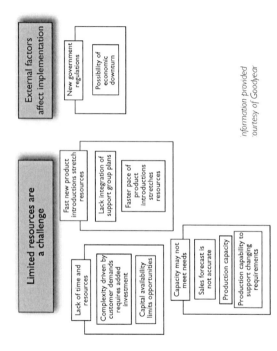

Information provided courtesy of Goodyear

NOTE: The Affinity helped the team bring focus to the many opinions on business planning. The headers that surfaced became the key issues in the ID example (shown in the ID tool section).

Affinity

Issues in generating reports from current operating system

Training

- Staff needs to be trained on software
- Need to understand input requirements for all audit programs
- No training manuals for the technology being used
- Only one subject matter expert on existing software

Technology

- Need more information added to database?
- Can't pull required information from the system now
- Something wrong with current database?
- Inputting data is a problem—not all information put in
- Limited intro
- Remote access to wireless is not universal

Technology

- Historic data not in the system
- Reports being generated in database have low credibility with staff
- Generating reports not user friendly
- Making report changes not user friendly
- Insufficient information to generate new reports (need new fields)

Roles & responsibilities

- Team members not taking ownership & responsibility for outcomes
- Lack of common understanding of who does what
- Need for system of supervising review and approval
- Some supervisors are reluctant to delegate to new staff
- One individual responsible for too many programs
- Declining support from business support unit

Procedures

- Inputting data is time consuming
- Timing of putting data in the system is not consistent
- Lost manual files have no backup
- Lack of storage for hard-copy files
- Information on clients in "collections" folder is not linked
- No revenue management system

Information provided courtesy of Province of Nova Scotia, Canada

Affinity

Improve service delivery to clients

Build excellence

- Develop work areas and individuals as experts
- Know who our experts are, and use them as experts
- Increase the diversity of service-related research
- Empower service-delivery teams
- Allow greater freedom of thought
- Increase external interactions
- Restore a rigorous peer-review culture

Review and improve processes

- Streamline processes for service delivery
- Identify service delivery bottlenecks
- Simplify internal reporting processes
- Increase clerical support to service delivery staff
- Reduce administrative overhead
- Benchmark our service delivery to measure achievement

Improve internal and external communications

- Teach report-writing skills to staff
- Improve stakeholder communications
- Simplify terminology and use less jargon
- Increase interaction within our organization
- Don't organize people into 'stovepipes'
- Share knowledge to reduce duplication of effort

Improve service delivery

- Define our services clearly to clients
- Align our services with client requirements
- Deliver what we say we will deliver
- Build relationships with clients
- Make staff individually responsible for deliverables
- Ensure our services remain relevant
- Market our services to new customers

Information provided courtesy of Australian Army

Affinity

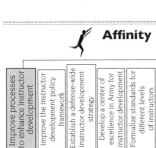

Improve the quality of our instructors

Improve the quality of our people

- Establish benchmarks for instructor knowledge and skills
- Develop 'Master' instructors to mentor and coach other instructors
- Bring in the best trainers (commercial or military) to train instructors
- Increase on-the-job training and development
- Support instructors in personal development and higher education
- Get instructors to identify their development needs
- Provide a career continuum for instructors

Improve the technology of instruction

- Broaden the range of instructional techniques and technology
- Give instructors advanced technology tools
- Develop a rich-media web site solely for sharing instructional ideas
- Improve the quality of simulators to enable practice by students
- Develop web-based computer-aided instruction for instructors
- Seek to participate in research on instructional technology

Improve incentives for instructors

- Link instructor development to a continuum of instructional standards and recognize/reward as appropriate
- Provide incentives (bonuses) based on performance assessments
- Increase the tenure of good instructors
- Recognize instructors as essential to the Army
- Reward skilled instructors with exchange postings to foreign countries

Improve processes to enhance instructor development

- Improve the instructor development policy framework
- Establish a defense-wide instructor development strategy
- Develop a center of excellence in Army for instructor development
- Formalize standards for different levels of instructors
- Develop a professional stream or trade structure for instructors
- Civilianize and professionalize the instructor trade
- Facilitate a virtual peer-support network

Information provided courtesy of Australian Army

Affinity

Improving interactions within headquarters

Identify IT improvements

- Enhance IT networks
- Increase use of video-conferencing
- Use electronic and virtual meeting tools
- Set up chat rooms and blogs

Develop process improvements

- Clearly define division of responsibilities
- Review business processes
- Start a project to improve communications
- Flatten the hierachy

Improve interpersonal communications

- Exchange staff between headquarters
- Conduct more liaison visits
- Facilitate lateral communication
- Conduct regular stakeholder meetings

Information provided courtesy of Australian Army

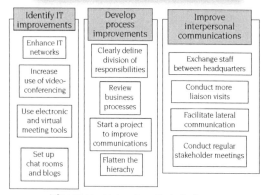

Issues associated with members obtaining well visits

Providers

- Too busy
- Not enough providers to meet demands
- Payor mix in commercial/ managed care
- Lack of tracking of who is due for well visit

Members

- Getting out of work
- Lack of transportation
- No incentive for healthy child
- Lack of awareness that child is due for care
- Lack of knowing what's available

Systems

- Unable to track who's due
- No geographical mapping software— network adequacy
- Claims data only good for recent visits
- Inaccurate member contact information from state during enrollment

Outreach

- Inability to contact due to inaccurate info. from members
- Inability to contact info. from state via enrollment files
- Outdated state files showing who is due, leading to inaccurate outreach
- Limited number of outreach staff for outreach calls

Information provided courtesy of Cook Children's Health Plan

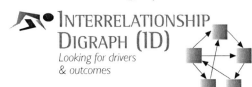

INTERRELATIONSHIP DIGRAPH (ID)
Looking for drivers & outcomes

Why use it?

To allow a team to systematically identify, analyze, and classify the cause-and-effect relationships that exist among all critical issues so that key drivers or outcomes can become the heart of an effective solution.

What does it do?

- ○ Encourages team members to think in multiple directions rather than linearly
- ○ Explores the cause-and-effect relationships among all the issues, including the most controversial
- ○ Allows the key issues to emerge naturally rather than allowing the issues to be forced by a dominant or powerful team member
- ○ Systematically surfaces the basic assumptions and reasons for disagreements among teams
- ○ Allows a team to identify root cause(s) even when credible data doesn't exist

How do I do it?

> What are the issues related to reducing litter?

1. **Agree on the issue/problem statement.**
   - ○ If using an original statement (it didn't come from a previous tool or discussion), create a

complete sentence that is clearly understood and
agreed on by team members.

○ If using input from other tools (such as an Affinity
Diagram), make sure that the goal under discussion is still the same and clearly understood.

2. Assemble the right team.

○ The ID requires more intimate knowledge of the
subject under discussion than is needed for the
Affinity. This is important if the final cause-and-
effect patterns are to be credible.

○ The ideal team size is generally 4–6 people. However, this number can be increased as long as the
issues are still visible and the meeting is well facili-
tated to encourage participation and maintain focus.

3. Lay out all of the ideas/issue cards that have either been brought from other tools or brainstormed.

○ Arrange 5–25 cards or notes in a large circular
pattern, leaving as much space as possible for
drawing arrows. Use large, bold printing, including a large number or letter on each idea for quick
reference later in the process.

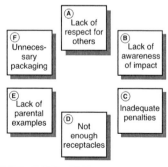

4. **Look for cause/influence relationships between all of the ideas, and draw relationship arrows.**
  ○ Choose any of the ideas as a starting point. If all of the ideas are numbered or lettered, work through them in sequence.
  ○ An outgoing arrow from an idea indicates that it is the stronger cause or influence.

Ask of each combination:
1) Is there a cause/influence relationship?
2) If yes, which direction of cause/influence is stronger?

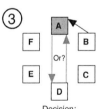

Decision: "B" causes or influences "A"

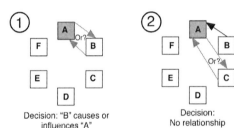

Decision: No relationship

Decision: No relationship

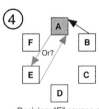

Decision: "E" causes or influences "A"

Continued on next page

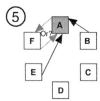

Decision:
No relationship.
"A" is completed.

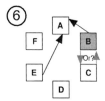

**Now begin with "B" and repeat
the questions for all remaining
combinations.**
Decision: "B" causes or
influences "C."

Draw only one-way relationship arrows in the direction of the
stronger cause or influence. Make a decision on the stronger
direction. *Do not draw two-headed arrows.*

5. Review and revise the first-round ID.

○ Get additional input from people who are not on
the team to confirm or modify the team's work.
Either bring the paper version to others or repro-
duce it using available software. Use a different
size print or a color marker to make additions or
deletions.

6. Tally the number of outgoing and incoming arrows, and select key items for further planning.

○ Record and clearly mark next to each issue the
number of arrows going in and out of it.

○ Find the item(s) with the highest number of *outgoing arrows* and the item(s) with the highest number
of *incoming arrows*.

○ *Outgoing arrows.* A high number of outgoing arrows
indicates an item that is a root cause or driver. This
is *generally* the issue that teams tackle first.

○ *Incoming arrows.* A high number of incoming arrows indicates an item that is a key outcome. This can become a focus for planning either as a meaningful measure of overall success or as a redefinition of the original issue under discussion.

Use common sense when you select the most critical issues to focus on. Issues with very close tallies must be reviewed carefully, but in the end, it is a judgment call, not science.

7. **Draw the final ID.**

○ Identify visually both the *key drivers* (greatest number of outgoing arrows) and the *key outcomes* (greatest number of incoming arrows). Typical methods are double boxes or bold boxes.

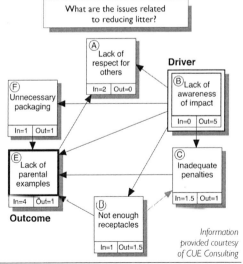

What are the issues related to reducing litter?

Ⓐ Lack of respect for others
In=2 | Out=0

Driver
Ⓑ Lack of awareness of impact
In=0 | Out=5

Ⓕ Unnecessary packaging
In=1 | Out=1

Ⓔ Lack of parental examples
In=4 | Out=1

Outcome

Ⓒ Inadequate penalties
In=1.5 | Out=1

Ⓓ Not enough receptacles
In=1 | Out=1.5

Information provided courtesy of CUE Consulting

Variations

When it is necessary to create a more orderly display of all of the relationships, a matrix format is very effective. The vertical (up) arrow is a driving cause, and the horizontal (side) arrow is an effect. The example below has added symbols indicating the strength of the relationships.

The "total" column is the sum of all of the "relationship strengths" in each row. This shows that you are working on those items that have the strongest effect on the greatest number of issues.

ID – Matrix Format

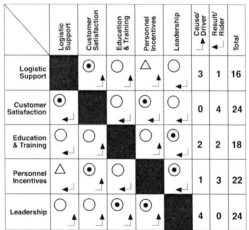

	Logistic Support	Customer Satisfaction	Education & Training	Personnel Incentives	Leadership	Cause/ Driver ▲	Result/ Rider ◄	Total
Logistic Support		⊙	◯	△	◯	3	1	16
Customer Satisfaction	⊙		◯	⊙	◯	0	4	24
Education & Training	◯	◯		◯	⊙	2	2	18
Personnel Incentives	△	⊙	◯		⊙	1	3	22
Leadership	◯	◯	⊙	⊙		4	0	24

Relationship Strength

⊙ = 9 Significant
◯ = 3 Medium
△ = 1 Weak

Information provided courtesy of U.S. Air Force, Air Combat Command

Interrelationship Digraph

Issues Surrounding
Implementation of the Business Plan

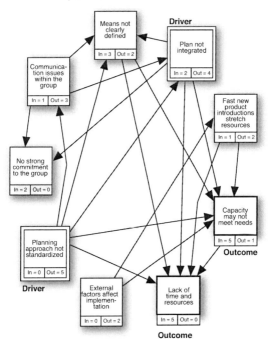

Information provided courtesy of Goodyear

NOTE: "The drivers" from this ID will be used as the goal in the Tree example shown at the end of the Tree Diagram/PDPC section.

Interrelationship Digraph

A Vision of Andover in the 21st Century

See next page for close up

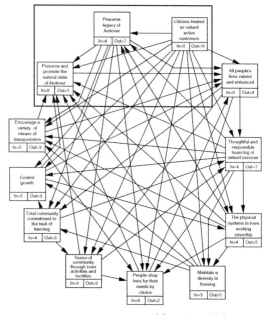

Preserve legacy of Andover	In=4	Out=7
Citizens treated as valued active customers	In=0	Out=11
Preserve and promote the natural state of Andover	In=9	Out=1
All people's lives valued and enhanced	In=6	Out=4
Encourage a variety of means of transportation	In=5	Out=3
Thoughtful and responsible financing of valued services	In=4	Out=7
Control growth	In=5	Out=3
Total community commitment to the task of learning	In=4	Out=3
The physical systems in town working smoothly	In=4	Out=5
Sense of community through town activities and facilities	In=4	Out=3
People shop here for their needs by choice	In=6	Out=2
Maintain a diversity in housing	In=3	Out=5

Information provided courtesy of Town of Andover, MA

Interrelationship Digraph

A Vision of Andover
in the 21st Century

Close up

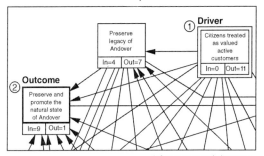

*Information provided courtesy
of Town of Andover, MA*

① This is the driver. If the focus on the citizen as a customer becomes the core of the town's vision, then everything else will be advanced.

② This is the primary outcome. It puts the preservation of nature in the town as a key indicator of the vision working.

Interrelationship Digraph

Improve turnaround time of morning lab results

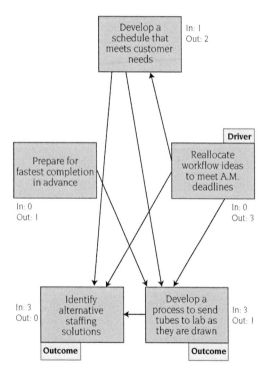

Interrelationship Digraph

Reduce turnaround time for EKGs

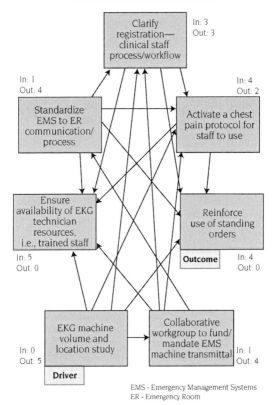

EMS - Emergency Management Systems
ER - Emergency Room

Information provided courtesy of Concord Hospital

PRIORITIZATION MATRICES
Weighing your options

	a	b	c

Why use it?

To narrow down options through a systematic approach of comparing choices by selecting, weighting, and applying criteria.

What does it do?

- ○ Quickly surfaces basic disagreements so they may be resolved up front
- ○ Forces a team to focus on the best thing(s) to do, and not everything they could do, dramatically increasing the chances for implementation success
- ○ Limits "hidden agendas" by surfacing the criteria as a necessary part of the process
- ○ Increases the chance of follow-through because consensus is sought at each step in the process (from criteria to conclusions)
- ○ Reduces the chances of selecting someone's "pet project"

How do I do it?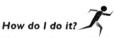

There are three methods for constructing Prioritization Matrices. The outline that follows indicates typical situations for using each method. Only the "Full Analytical Criteria Method" is discussed here. The others are covered fully in *The Memory Jogger Plus+*®.

Full Analytical Criteria Method

Typically used when:

- Smaller teams are involved (3–8 people)
- Options are few (5–10 choices)
- There are relatively few criteria (3–6 items)
- Complete consensus is needed
- The stakes are high if the plan fails

Consensus Criteria Method

This method follows the same steps as in the Full Analytical Criteria Method except the Consensus Criteria Method uses a combination of weighted voting, and ranking is used instead of paired comparisons.

Typically used when:

- Larger teams are involved (8 or more people)
- Options are many (10–20 choices)
- There is a significant number of criteria (6–15 items)
- Quick consensus is needed to proceed

Combination ID/Matrix Method

This method is different from the other two methods because it is based on cause and effect, rather than criteria.

Typically used when:

- Interrelationships among options are high and finding the option with the greatest impact is critical

Full Analytical Criteria Method

1. Agree on the ultimate goal to be achieved in a clear, concise sentence.

- If no other tools are used as input, produce a clear goal statement through consensus. This statement strongly affects which criteria are used.

> Choose the most enjoyable vacation
> for the whole family

2. Create the list of criteria.

- Brainstorm the list of criteria or review previous documents or guidelines that are available (e.g., corporate goals, budget-related guidelines).

> • Cost
> • Educational value
> • Diverse activity
> • Escape reality

 The team must reach consensus on the final criteria and their meanings, or the process is likely to fail!

3. Using an L-shaped matrix, weight each criterion against each other.

- Reading across from the vertical axis, compare each criterion to those on the horizontal axis.
- Each time a weight (e.g., 1, 5, 10) is recorded in a row cell, its reciprocal value (e.g., $\frac{1}{5}$, $\frac{1}{10}$) must be recorded in the corresponding column cell.
- Total each horizontal row and convert to a relative decimal value known as the "criteria weighting."

Criterion vs. Criterion

Criteria \ Criteria	Cost	Educ. value	Diverse activity	Escape reality	Row Total	Relative Decimal Value
Cost		$\frac{1}{5}$	$\frac{1}{10}$	5	5.3	.15
Educ. value	5		$\frac{1}{5}$	5	10.2	.28
Diverse activity	10	5		5	20	.55
Escape reality	$\frac{1}{5}$	$\frac{1}{5}$	$\frac{1}{5}$		.60	.02
				Grand Total	36.1	

1 = Equally important
5 = More important
10 = Much more important
$\frac{1}{5}$ = Less important
$\frac{1}{10}$ = Much less important

Row Total
Rating scores added
Grand Total
Row totals added
Relative Decimal Value
Each row total ÷ by the grand total

4. Compare ALL options relative to each weighted criterion.

○ For each criterion, create an L-shaped matrix with all of the options on both the vertical and horizontal axes and the criteria listed in the lefthand corner of the matrix. **There will be as many options matrices as there are criteria to be applied.**

○ Use the same rating scale (1, 5, 10) as in Step 3, BUT customize the wording for each criterion.

○ The relative decimal value is the "option rating."

Options vs. Each Criterion (Cost Criterion)

Cost	Disney World	Gettys-burg	New York City	Uncle Henry's	Row Total	Relative Decimal Value
Disney World		$\frac{1}{5}$	5	$\frac{1}{10}$	5.3	.12
Gettys-burg	5		10	$\frac{1}{5}$	15.2	.33
New York City	$\frac{1}{5}$	$\frac{1}{10}$		$\frac{1}{10}$	.40	.01
Uncle Henry's	10	5	10		25	.54
				Grand Total	45.9	

1 = Equal cost
5 = Less expensive
10 = Much less expensive
$^1/_5$ = More expensive
$^1/_{10}$ = Much more expensive

Continue Step 4 through three more Options/Criterion matrices, like this:

Escape reality

Crt.	Options			
Options				

Diverse activity

Crt.	Options			
Options				

Educational value

Crt.	Options			
Options				

The whole number (1, 5, 10) must always represent a desirable rating. In some cases this may mean "less" (e.g., cost); in others this may mean "more" (e.g., tasty).

5. **Using an L-shaped summary matrix, compare each option based on all criteria combined.**

   ○ List all criteria on the horizontal axis and all options on the vertical axis.

   ○ In each matrix cell multiply the "criteria weighting" of each criterion (decimal value from Step 3) by the "option rating" (decimal value from Step 4). This creates an "option score."

   ○ Add each option score across all criteria for a row total. Divide each row total by the grand total and convert to the final decimal value. Compare these decimal values to help you decide which option to pursue.

Summary Matrix
Options vs. All Criteria

Criteria Optns.	Cost (.15)	Educa- tional value (.28)	Diverse activity (.55)	Escape reality (.02)	Row Total	Relative Decimal Value (RT √ GT)
Disney World	.12 x .15 (.02)	.24 x .28 (.07)	.40 x .55 (.22)	.65 x .02 (.01)	.32	.32
Gettys- burg	.33 x .15 (.05)	.37 x .28 (.10)	.10 x .55 (.06)	.22 x .02 (0)	.22	.22
New York City	.01 x .15 (0)	.37 x .28 (.10)	.49 x .55 (.27)	.12 x .02 (0)	.37	.38
Uncle Henry's	.54 x .15 (.08)	.01 x .28 (0)	.01 x .55 (.01)	.01 x .02 (0)	.09	.09
				Grand Total	1.00	

.54   x   .15
(from Step 4 matrix)   (from Step 3 matrix)

(.08)
Option score

6. Choose the best option(s) across all criteria.

 While this is more systematic than traditional decision making, it is not a science. Use common sense and judgment when options are rated very closely, but be open to nontraditional conclusions.

Variations

See *The Memory Jogger Plus+*® for full explanations of both the Consensus Criteria Method and the Combination ID/Matrix Method. The Full Analytical Criteria Method, illustrated in this book, is recommended because it encourages full discussion and consensus on critical issues. The Full Analytical Criteria Method is a simplified adaptation of an even more rigorous model known as the Analytical Hierarchy Process. It is based on the work of Thomas Saaty, which he describes in his book *Decision Making for Leaders*. In any case, use common sense to know when a situation is important enough to warrant such thorough processes.

Prioritization

Choosing a Standard
Corporate Spreadsheet Program

① Weighting criteria (described in Step 3)

This is a portion of a full matrix with 14 criteria in total.

Criteria	Best use of hardware	Ease of use	Maximum functionality	Best performance	Total (14 criteria)	Relative decimal value
Best use of hardware		.20	.10	.20	3.7	.01
Ease of use	5.0		.20	.20	35.4	.08
Maximum functionality	10.0	5.0		5.0	69.0	.17
Best performance	5.0	5.0	.20		45.2	.11
			Grand Total (14 criteria)		418.1	

Information provided courtesy of Novacor Chemicals

NOTE: This constructed example, illustrated on three pages, represents only a portion of the prioritization process and only a portion of Novacor's spreadsheet evaluation process. Novacor Chemicals assembled a 16-person team, composed mainly of system users and some information systems staff. The team developed and weighted 14 standard criteria and then applied them to choices in word processing, spreadsheet, and presentation graphics programs.

This example continued on the next page

② Comparing options (described in Step 4)

These are just 2 of 14 matrices.

Best integration –internal	Program A	Program B	Program C	Total	Relative decimal value
Program A		1.00	1.00	2.00	.33
Program B	1.00		1.00	2.00	.33
Program C	1.00	1.00		2.00	.33
			Grand Total	6.00	

Lowest ongoing cost	Program A	Program B	Program C	Total	Relative decimal value
Program A		.10	.20	.30	.02
Program B	10.00		5.00	15.00	.73
Program C	5.00	.20		5.20	.25
			Grand Total	20.50	

Information provided courtesy of Novacor Chemicals

This example continued on the next page

Prioritization

Choosing a Standard
Corporate Spreadsheet Program (cont.)

③ Summarize option ratings across all criteria
(described in Step 5)

This is a portion of a full matrix with 14 criteria in total.

Criteria Options	Easy to use (.08)	Best integration int. (.09)	Lowest ongoing cost (.08)	Total (across 14 criteria)	Relative decimal value
Program A	.03 (.01)	.33 (.03)	.02 (0)	.16	.18
Program B	.48 (.04)	.33 (.03)	.73 (.06)	.30	.33
Program C	.48 (.04)	.33 (.03)	.25 (.02)	.44	.49
			Grand Total	.90	

Information provided courtesy of Novacor Chemicals

RESULT: Program C was chosen. Even though 14 out of the 16 team members were not currently using this program, the prioritization process changed their minds and prevented them from biasing the final decision.

Index

NOTE:

Bold page ranges indicate significant discussions for that topic.